BOOK 3 Breeding Aquarium Fishes

by dr. herbert r. axelrod and lourdes burgess

Distributed in the U.S.A. by T.F.H. Publications, Inc., 211 West Sylvania Avenue, P.O. Box 27, Neptune City, N.J. 07753; in England by T.F.H. (Gt. Britain) Ltd., 13 Nutley Lane, Reigate, Surrey; in Canada by Clarke, Irwin & Company, Clarwin House, 791 St. Clair Avenue West, Toronto 10, Ontario; in Southeast Asia by Y. W. Ong, 9 Lorong 36 Geylang, Singapore 14; in Australia and the south Pacific by Pet Imports Pty. Ltd., P.O. Box 149, Brookvale 2100, N.S.W., Australia.
Published by T.F.H. Publications, Inc. Ltd., The British Crown Colony of Hong Kong.

Cover Photo by Hans Joachim Richter.

© 1973 by T.F.H. Publications, Inc. Ltd.

TABLE OF CONTENTS

The Nyasa Golden Cichlid,
    Pseudotropheus auratus 7
Fuelleborn's Cichlid,
    Labeotropheus fuelleborni 25
Griem's Tetra,
    Hyphessobrycon griemi 46
The Blue Convict Cichlid,
    Cichlasoma spilurum 57
The Black Tetra,
    Gymnocorymbus ternetzi 67
The Sierra Leone Cichlid,
    Pelmatochromis thomasi 84
The Pearl Danio,
    Brachydanio albolineata 92
The Five-banded Barb,
    Barbodes pentazona 101
The Jewel Cichlid,
    Hemichromis bimaculatus II 114
The Golden Rasbora,
    Rasbora daniconius 143
The Chocolate Gourami,
    Sphaerichthys osphromenoides 154
The Red Top Cichlid,
    Labeotropheus trewavasae 185
Goldfish,
    Carassius auratus 197
The Chanchito,
    Cichlasoma facetum 216
The Cuban Rivulus,
    Rivulus cylindraceus 225
The Guppy,
    Poecilia reticulata 237
The Tiger or Zebra Cichlid,
    Tilapia mariae 266
The Indian Glass Fish,
    Chanda ranga 279
American Flagfish,
    Jordanella floridae 289
Schaller's Gourami,
    Trichopsis schalleri 296
The Burundi Killy,
    Aphyosemion scheeli 313

INTRODUCTION

About ten years ago, while on a lecture tour in Brno, Czechoslovakia, I ended up after one of the talks drinking beer with a group of Hungarians, Czechs, Poles and East Germans until the wee hours of the morning. One big, smiling East German kept telling me about his escapades in spawning this and that fish, until finally, in a blast of self-esteem he whispered . . . "I also spawned the Chocolate Gourami on several occasions."

This was too much for me. I didn't believe a word this fellow said. "What's your name," I asked?

"Hans Joachim Richter," he said. "But my friends call me Jochen."

"O. K. Jochen. If you're so good, why don't you take pictures of your spawning feats and prove to the world how great you are!"

"I will!"

He did.

At the present time, Hans Joachim Richter of Leipzig, DDR is the world's best aquarium fish photographer. Without exception. His photographs are so detailed and so vital in the information they record that I have selected a few of his best for the front and back covers of this book, and the photograph on the facing page is just a sample of the kind of photo taken by Jochen for Book 4 in this series of BREEDING AQUARIUM FISHES.

Herbert R. Axelrod

Julidochromis ornatus. Photo by H. J. Richter.

Nyasa Golden Cichlid
Pseudotropheus auratus Boulenger

The Nyasa Golden Cichlid is one of the smaller fishes from Lake Malawi (formerly called Nyasa) and one of the Great Lakes of Africa. This fish together with other fishes inhabiting the shore area of the lake are collectively called mbuna (pronounced *em-boo-na*) by the natives. The climate in this large lake with an area of about 11,500 sq. mi. and a depth of about 2,300 feet is hot and humid. The water temperature remains about 72°F. or higher throughout the year. Due to hydrographic conditions peculiar to the lake the water is unusually clear to a depth of about 65 feet. This mbuna inhabits the rocky and sandy areas of the lake where some green plants, mostly *Vallisneria*, are growing. These conditions have to be considered if one is to keep and breed the *auratus* successfully.

P. auratus is an aggressive fish but this is probably the quality sought by some hobbyists more than the attractive appearance it presents.

As a species the Nyasa Golden Cichlid is not difficult to recognize. It has a basic golden yellow color traversed by 2 or 3 deep black stripes each one edged by a glistening blue line. The tail has a few large dots. The female has 3 longitudinal stripes including one along the dorsal fin which is absent in the male whose dorsal fin is clear and whose ventral side becomes very dark to deep black during breeding time. The male also has a vivid orange spot on the anal fin which does not appear among the females. However identifiying the sexes is not that simple because either sex may appear dark or light depending not only on the sexual condition but also on the physiological state. One confirms the sex by observing the relative size of the abdomen and the genital papilla. A mature female has a slightly swollen abdomen and

The dark bands of the female *P. auratus* are usually edged by iridescent blue lines which may appear faded depending on the physiological and psychological state of the fish. Photo by Dr. H. R. Axelrod.

a few days prior to spawning the genital papilla is extended and distinctly visible.

Due to their aggressive nature these fishes require large tanks of 40 to 60 gallons capacity or larger. Hiding places could be provided by placing rocks (preferably slate) as decoration and an ample amount of plants like *Vallisneria* or any bushy type. Water at a temperature of 78° to 80°, soft and neutral to slightly alkaline is ideal. Enough light to encourage the growth of algae on the rocks and walls of the tank is desirable. Algae and detrital matter is continually nibbled by them. They will not hesitate taking blood worms, *Tubifex, Daphnia,* and even cooked shrimp and mussels.

They should be preferably maintained in a tank by themselves or only with larger species. They are very territorial and develop hierarchies among themselves in the tank. Any new addition is quickly challenged and sometimes slain.

Males of equal strength indulge in mouth to mouth tug of war with no apparent harm to each other however.

For spawning purposes a smaller tank of about 20 gallons or less will be sufficient but it should have plenty of plants that are securely attached and a coarse gravel bottom with some flat rocks. A substrate of fine particles should be avoided for it can injure the eggs in the case where small rocks are taken in as the female picks the eggs from the bottom.

Females of this species may drop their eggs even in the absence of males. This is an indication of the ease with

Although the fry are capable of existing independently after leaving the brood pouch for the first time, they are usually taken back by the female *P. auratus* at night for the next few days. Photo by A. F. Orsini.

which they spawn. They can spawn in the community tank but for convenience and protection of the female and young it is advisable to provide special quarters for them.

Once a male and female are together the typical cichlid courtship occurs. This is quite stormy in *P. auratus*. If the female is not ready she should be removed before she is fatally injured. The male besides being territorial of his chosen area also digs pits in the bottom or cleans the rocky surfaces of the rocks at the approach of spawning time. Spawning occurs immediately after a brief courtship. With their first encounter, the male approaches the female from

A female *Pseudotropheus auratus*. This species is common to the shores of Lake Malawi and is one of the most attractive members of the mbuna. Photo by H. Hansen.

Color changes occur dramatically in *P. auratus* especially among the males during breeding time. The third dorsal dark band is normally a characteristic of the female fish. Photo by G. Marcuse.

the rear, followed by a series of movements describing a left- or right-handed circle. Then, for a few moments, either the male or the female assumes a position forming a **T** in relation to the other. The head is directed towards the genital or anal area of the other and with the accompaniment of a series of quivers both partners release their reproductive products. The female after laying 3–6 eggs very close to the bottom, picks them up with her mouth immediately and the ritual of spawning is started all over again. Whenever the female assumes the **T** position her mouth is close to the

The highly specialized mouth parts of *P. auratus* are adapted for very efficiently scraping off the algae growing on the rocks. However, these fish also may feed on other types of food. Photo by W. Hoppe.

(On facing page). During breeding time the darker *P. auratus* male can change to almost solid black with contrasting electric blue bands whereas the female often maintains the bright golden yellow coloration with three solid black bands. Note her distended throat pouch. Photo by Dr. D. Terver.

Note the egg-like spots on the hind part of the anal fin of this adult male *P. auratus*. Photo by H. Hansen.

A male *P. auratus* apparently quite aware of the female above about to enter his "territory". Visual signals play an important role in their spawning behavior. Photo by Dr. D. Terver.

(Above and below). A male *P. auratus* in his den. Bright and conspicuous coloration is considered as a warning signal not only to members of the same species but also to other species as well that *"this is my domain and keep off"*. Photos by Dr. D. Terver.

A brooding female *P. auratus* is easily recognized by the distended throat. During this period food is not taken and some loss of weight may be noticed. Photo by A. F. Orsini.

Like most territorial cichlids, an adult male *P. auratus*, shown here in its breeding color pattern, is usually aggressive and when in the company of other fishes should be maintained in large aquaria with sufficient hiding places. Photo by G. Marcuse.

Eggs of *P. auratus* three days after fertilization. They are gently rounded at one end and pointed on the opposite end, shaped like a pear. They measure about 3 mm in length and the yellow colored yolk is visible through the transparent egg membrane. The eggs are carefully picked up immediately after they are laid and incubated within the mouth cavity of the female fish. Photo by Dr. D. Terver.

Frontal confrontation between two male *P. auratus* may or may not lead to direct body contact when jaw-pulling and pushing do occur. Photo by Dr. D. Terver.

genital region of the male; since the eggs are in her mouth they are insured of being fertilized as the male releases his milt. It is presumed that the prominent spot on the anal fin of the male resembles an egg and as the female attempts to pick it up, she gets a mouthful of sperm, thus the eggs in her mouth will not escape being fertilized. Depending upon her size and age a female *P. auratus* may lay about 60 eggs.

The male, soon after the completion of spawning, should be removed or he will continue chasing the female who is

An incubating female *P. auratus* with a color pattern similar to that of a male. Such color change appears gradually and is presumed hormonal in origin. Photo by Dr. D. Terver.

Another incubating female *P. auratus* with the usual female color pattern. Photo by Dr. D. Terver.

visibly incubating the eggs in her buccal cavity by now. One should refrain from exciting or moving the female soon after spawning or during the early stages of incubation. While she could easily disgorge the developing eggs which can be damaged or lost, she will usually pick them up again if ever this happens. The length of incubation varies between 23 to 30 days after spawning with temperature and age of the spawners. Incubation is ended when the young

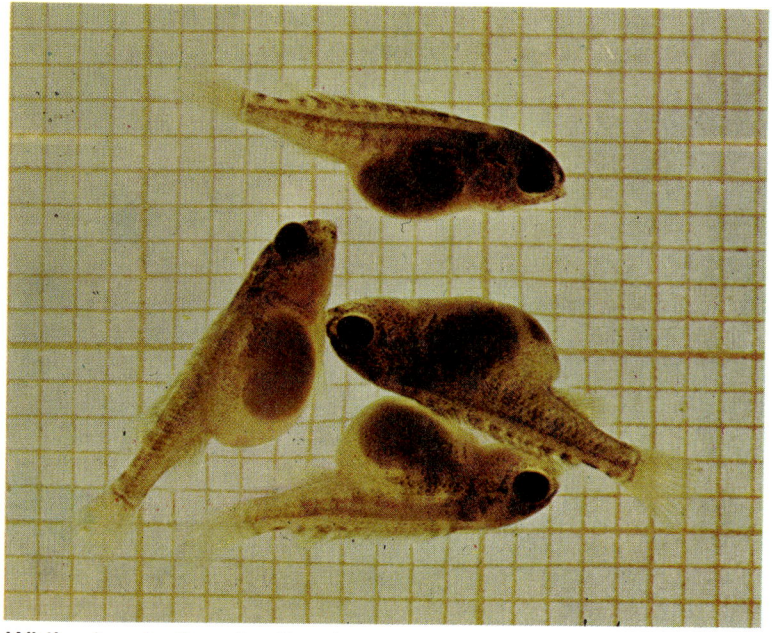

While incubating in the buccal pouch of the female the *Pseudotropheus* fry need not eat until the yolk sac is fully absorbed. Photo by G. Marcuse.

have lost their yolk sacs and are able to leave the mouth of the female. For the next 9 to 10 days she will instinctively collect them at night. During the early and greater part of the period of incubation a constant masticatory movement will be observed whereby the developing eggs are fanned or oxygenated. The female is not capable of eating during this stage but she will be able to eat normally once the fry are free swimming. She might eat much earlier if there are not too many fry inside the buccal cavity.

The fry at the time of their first emergence measure about 10 to 12 mm long. *P. auratus* grows slowly and attains

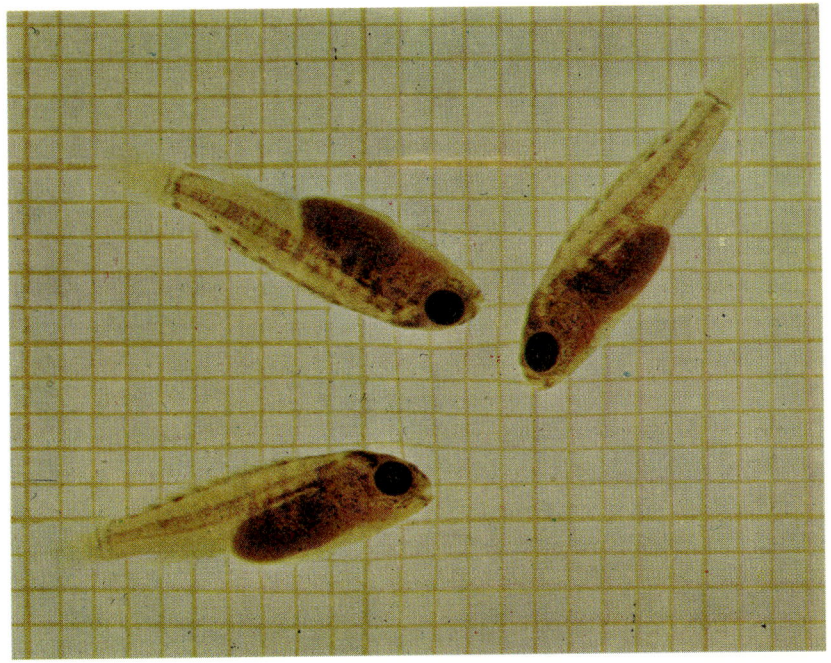

Pseudotropheus fry almost ready to leave the security of the buccal pouch and start living independently. These fry are hungry as their un-rounded bellies indicate. Photo by G. Marcuse.

sexual maturity in 13 months. They attain a length of 4 inches in captivity. The young can be safely kept with the female for as long as a month provided she is well fed.

Adult and young *P. auratus* are relatively hardy fish. They can withstand some variations in temperature, pH,

(Above and below). Two male *P. auratus* engaged in jaw-pushing. Such a "battle" does not end fatally for the weaker fish withdraws gracefully with very little damage. Photos by Dr. D. Terver.

The male and female *P. auratus* are distinct from each other not only in appearance but also in behavior during spawning so that retrieval of the male afterwards is relatively easy. Photo by A. F. Orsini.

The fry returning into the mouth of the female. Her willingness to accept the young diminishes after several days as the fry also become more independent. Photo by A. F. Orsini.

and water hardness much better than other fishes found in the same habitat. Understandably extreme lowering of the temperature will be detrimental to all species from the tropics.

Daphnia shown here much enlarged is one type of food eaten by many fishes including the mbunas. Photo by Dr. K. Knaack.

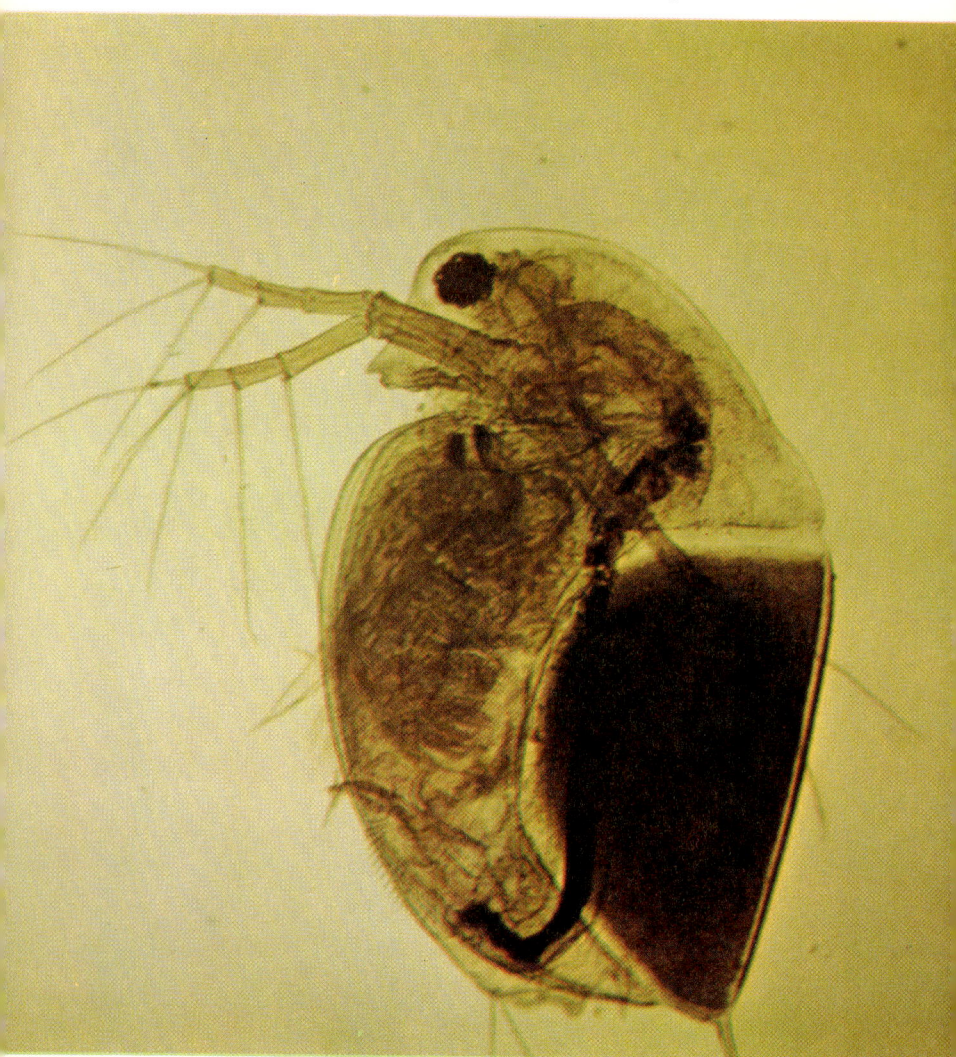

A view of Lake Malawi (formerly called Lake Nyasa) one of the rift lakes of Africa which supports the unique rock fish fauna called *mbuna*. Photo by Dr. David H. Eccles.

Fuelleborn's Cichlid

Labeotropheus fuelleborni Ahl

Labeotropheus fuelleborni is a member of the community of small sized fishes which are ecologically associated with the rocky shores of Lake Malawi, one of the rift lakes of Africa. The mbuna (em-boo-na) as the local people call the shore fishes represent a very interesting group of living things to the biologist, especially the evolutionists and ecologists.

A male and female *Labeotropheus fuelleborni* in the typical T-position a few moments prior to spawning. Photo by Dr. D. Terver.

Besides adequate hiding places a tank set up for *L. fuelleborni* should receive plenty of light to encourage algal growth which are nibbled constantly by this mbuna cichlid. Photo by S. Lieberman.

Due to a restricted area, in this case the rocky shores, available for exploitation by the different species of fish, different types of feeding mechanisms and life styles developed in order to lessen competition.

This mbuna is an algae eater and this habit is very well reflected in the characteristics of the mouth parts. The ventral position and horseshoe shape of the mouth, together with the broad, spatulate, and inwardly curved teeth, enable this fish to scrape the algae from the rocks very efficiently. This adaptation does not preclude their eating other types of food. In the aquarium they eat a great variety of food such as *Tubifex*, *Daphnia*, *Artemia*, cyclops, even cooked shrimp, mussel and beef heart. However, the females are usually not able to feed while they brood the young, since they carry both eggs and young in their mouths.

Labeotropheus fuelleborni, together with a few other Malawi cichlids, are particularly interesting on account of their polymorphism. Loosely defined polymorphism is the occurrence of several forms or types of individuals in a population; in this instance several color forms. This phenomenon is quite common in some families of insects but unusual among fishes. The males and females of most fish species are distinct from each other in coloration especially during breeding time; this is also true for this cichlid. Both sexes have the "normal" coloration and a pattern of a blue background with 6–8 dark vertical bands. The females appear lighter with a pale blue color with a greenish cast; her bands are less distinct and paler. A second dramatically different color form exists *among the females only*. These females are speckled with orange and dark brown instead of having bars. In spite of this color difference

Note the horseshoe shaped and ventrally located mouth of *L. fuelleborni* which is adapted for scraping the mats of filamentous algae growing on the surface of rocks. Photo by W. Hoppe.

A pair of courting *L. fuelleborni*. The fish on the right displaying with widely spread fins and heightened coloration. Photo by Müller-Schmida.

the speckled form is still an integral part of the species. Yellow to orange spots are present on the anal fin and posterior end of the dorsal fin of both sexes. These spots are the so-called "egg dummies" which according to behaviorists play an important role in cichlid reproduction. (See Dr. Wickler's book.)

Being a sensitive fish, *L. fuelleborni* reacts instantly to such stimuli as strong light, sudden movements, presence of other fishes, etc. and this reponse is indicated by quick color change. When a male fish is frightened, he turns very pale so that the cross bands become more striking. The adults and especially the fry are easily affected by changes in the water chemistry and thermal conditions during captivity. One must, therefore, keep the conditions in the aquarium relatively constant. They require a fairly large tank of 40 to 60 gallon capacity, larger if possible, water that is well aerated, plenty of light to encourage the growth of algae to satisfy their desire for plant food, enough hiding

The transverse stripes in individual *L. fuelleborni* can appear very prominent (above) or almost absent (below). Photos by G. Marcuse.

The much discussed anal fin spots found in some mouthbrooding cichlids are seen here not only on the anal fin but also on the dorsal fin of *L. fuelleborni*. Photo by H. Hansen.

places which is achieved by arranging the rock decorations in a manner whereby enough caves are created, some strongly anchored plants as *Vallisneria*, a coarse gravel bottom liberally scattered with flat surfaced stones like slate; and finally, a good supply of clean, clear, alkaline, soft water with a temperature of 72 to 80°F. Some aquarists maintain and spawn their mbunas in hard water (although the water of Lake Malawi is soft) as a means of controlling fungus disease.

Territoriality is an inherent trait among cichlids, not only during breeding time, but throughout their adult lives. This is expressed by some form of aggressiveness to all intruders. When several fish are placed in a tank for the first time each fish "stakes out his claim" and will protect his chosen site vigorously. A "pecking order" is established; the strongest fish gets the best position and so on down the line according to size and strength. Once established, the community stays fairly quiet except for a few mouth to

After the pre-spawning activities this pair of mouth-brooding *L. fuelleborni* will move closer to the bottom and spawn on top of a previously selected and cleaned site. Photo by S. Lieberman.

mouth battles between the males; the frequency of this sport increases with the approach of spawning, so it is not wise to introduce strange fish during this period particularly if space is limited. If a new *fuelleborni* or even a female from the same tank has to be returned, it is better to do this at night before the lights are turned off when direct confrontation may be avoided.

In preparation to spawning the male digs pits in the gravel and cleans the surface of the larger rocks about his territory. If the fish are ready, spawning may take place easily in the community tank. This is not desirable. The female should be provided with special quarters where she can incubate the eggs in peace. A smaller tank 20 gallons or less can serve as a spawning tank and, after the male is

Rapid changes in color and pattern of many mouth-brooders like *L. fuelleborni* are utilized as visual signals during fighting, courting and brooding. Photo by G. Marcuse.

removed, can serve as a rearing tank as well. The female has to be protected from the pursuit of ardent males for she might easily spit out the eggs.

It does not take long for spawning to occur as soon as the ripe male and female are together. An over-eager male can kill a female that is not ready so one has to be sure of her sexual condition. She is ready if, in addition to a slightly swollen abdomen, her genital papilla is visible. It protrudes to about 2 mm long a few days prior to spawning.

Courtship is turbulent to the extent of stirring up the bottom and uprooting plants. The actual shedding of the eggs and sperm is accompanied by much trembling of the body when the partners are in a position resembling that of a **T**. The usual cichlid spawning behavior of display and tail chasing in circular fashion has, of course, taken place earlier. The female picks up all the eggs as they are laid and the process of spawning is repeated several times. During the **T** position the head of either fish is held close to the vent of the other and whenever the female assumes this posture, the eggs in her mouth are assured of being fertilized. It is presumed this behavior is enhanced by the presence of the "egg dummies" in the anal fin of the male which act as a lure to move her head towards the vent of the male. She is supposed to think these spots are eggs, and in trying to snap them up she gets a mouthful of sperm.

The male should be removed as soon as the female appears to have picked up all the eggs. The pair shed about 50 eggs in this species depending upon the size and age of the female. She will not require any food for the next 23 to 30 days while she is incubating the young. Young *fuelleborni* are about 10 to 12 mm long when they leave the buccal pouch for the first time and are able to feed on small sized live or prepared food including very fine algae. For a week or thereabouts the fry can get in and out of the mouth of the female. They are usually kept in her mouth overnight. By this time she is capable of eating her young but if enough

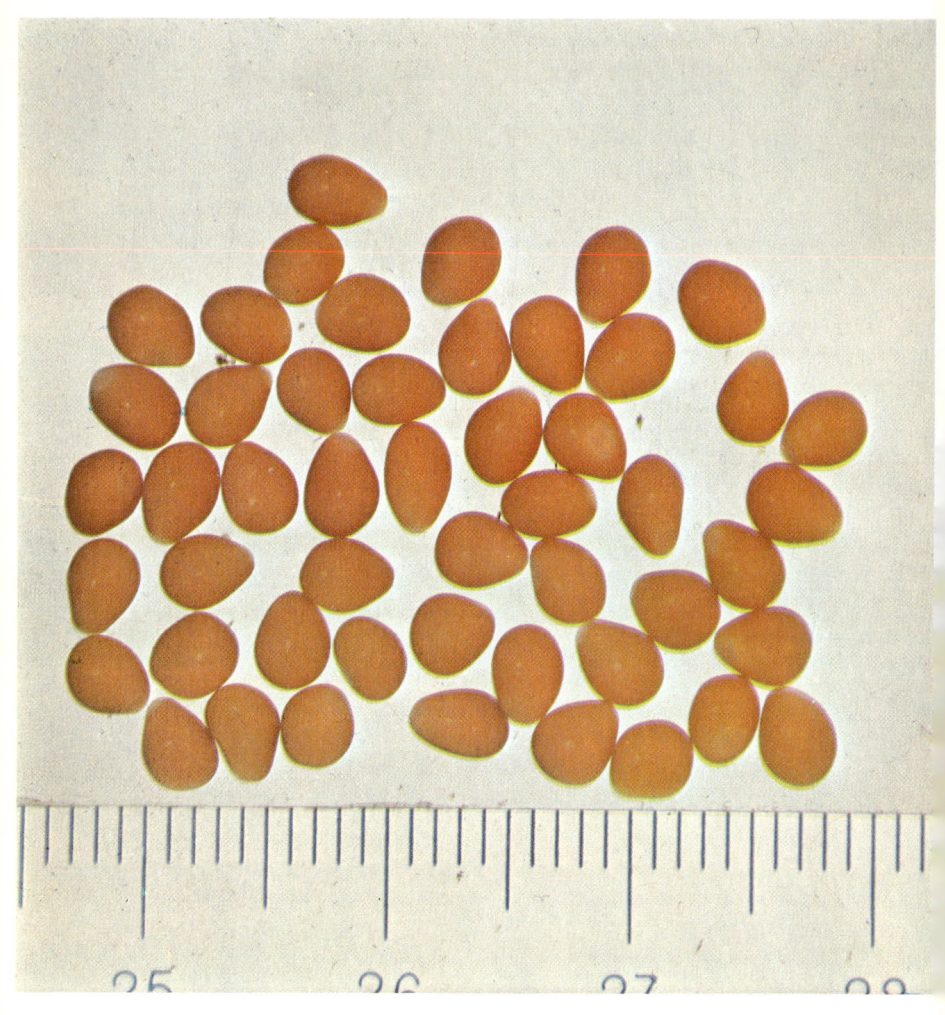

L. fuelleborni eggs magnified along with a millimeter scale for comparison. During incubation the developing young use the yolk comprising the greater bulk of the egg at this stage gradually. Photo by Dr. D. Terver.

Newly hatched fry of *L. fuelleborni* about 11 mm in length. They will eventually develop the barred pattern of the adults. Female speckled forms develop in a year or so during sexual differentiation. Photo by Dr. D. Terver.

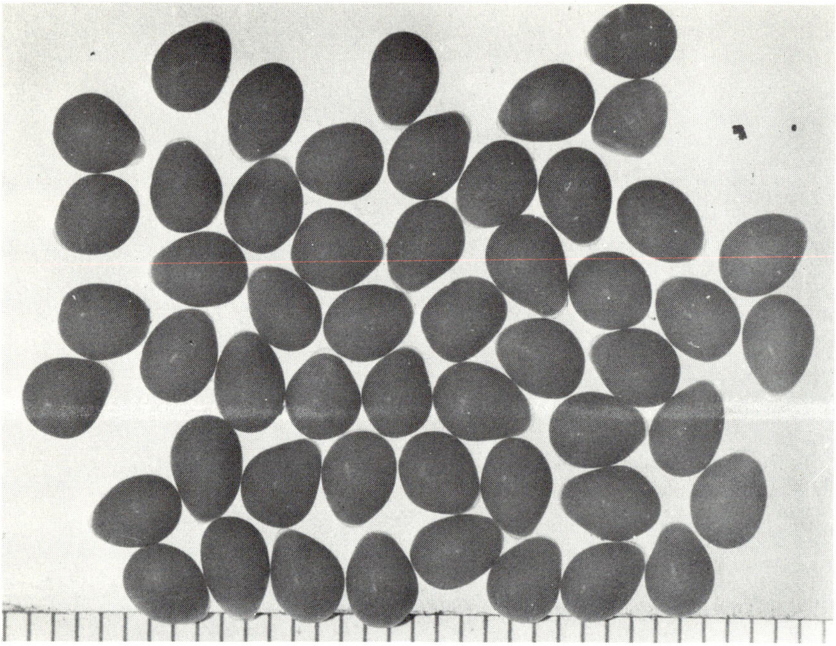

L. fuelleborni eggs 24 hours after fertilization and, below, after three days of incubation. Photos by Dr. D. Terver.

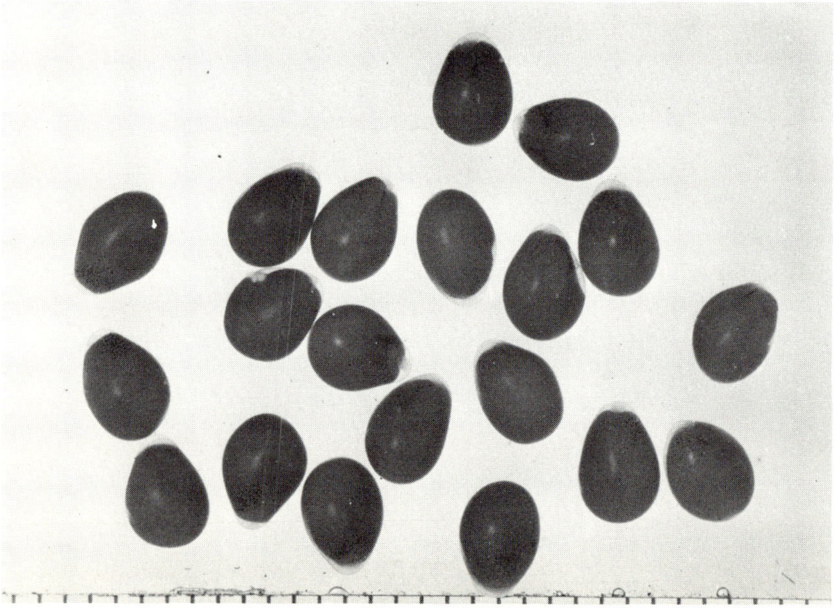

L. fuelleborni eggs after four days of incubation and, below, after six days of incubation. By this period the eyes are already formed. Photos by Dr. D. Terver.

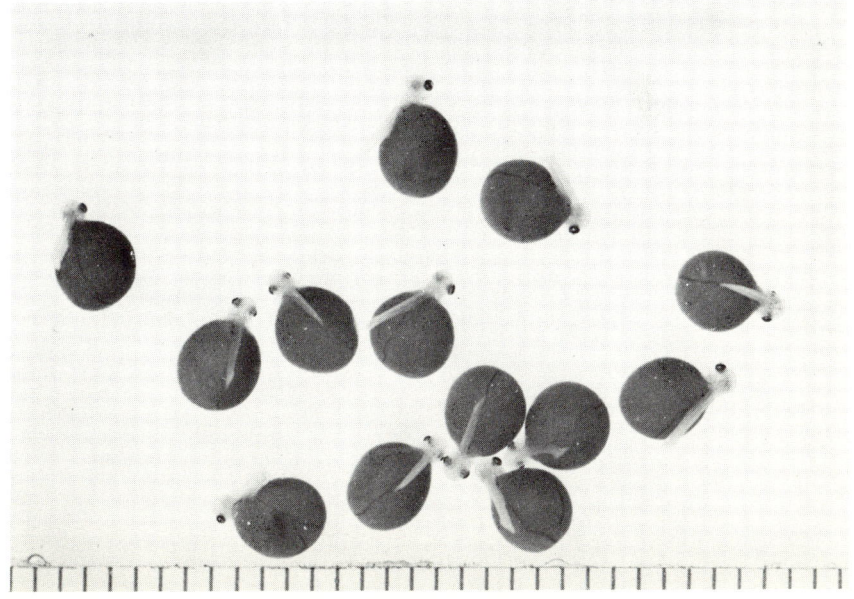

The iridescent blue cast of the adult is already evident in these 13 mm long fry of *L. fuelleborni*. They can now swim freely and are able to feed on small sized live food. Photo by Dr. D. Terver.

food is offered they can stay with the mother for as long as a month. The young tend to stay in the darker areas of the tank.

The fry grow slowly and full development of the ventrally located mouth takes about 3 months. All the fry resemble the barred adult pattern. Speckled forms may appear in about a year, when sexual dimorphism is recognizable. Adults measure about 4–5 inches and at an age of 13 months they are ready to spawn.

A close view of a young *L. fuelleborni* (6 days after leaving the buccal pouch for the first time). The terminal mouth of the fry is transformed into the ventrally positioned mouth of the adults, below, three months later. Photos by Stanley Lieberman.

L. fuelleborni eggs after seven days of incubation and below, after eight days of incubation. The head pigments are clearly seen and the yolk sac is slightly smaller. Photos by Dr. D. Terver.

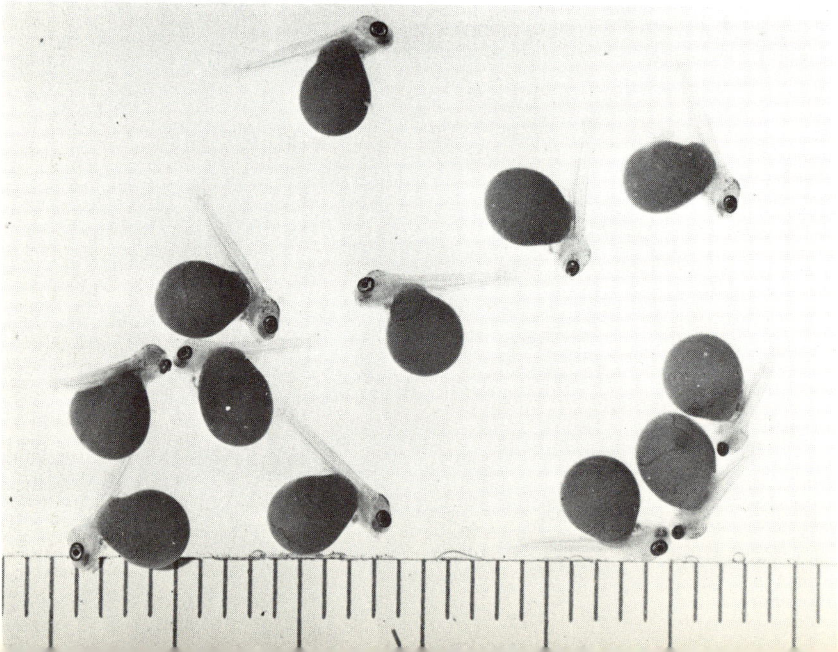

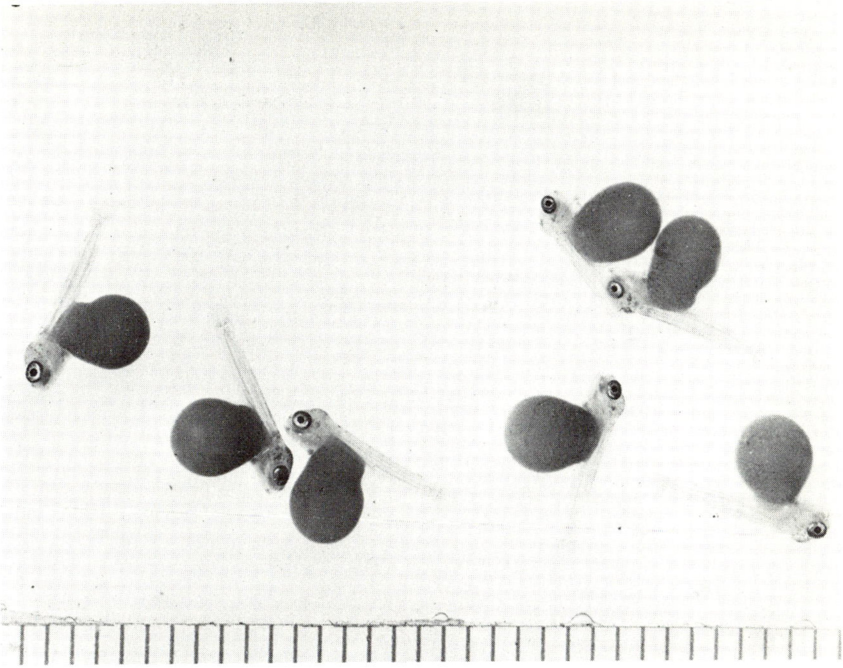

L. fuelleborni eggs after nine days of incubation and below, after 11 days of incubation. Some of the body pigments are now very apparent. Photos by Dr. D. Terver.

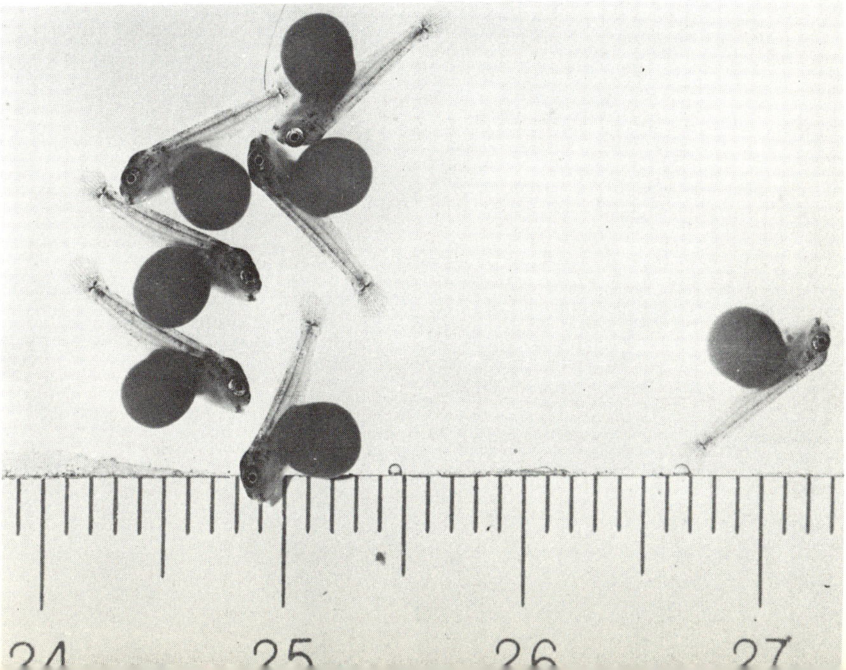

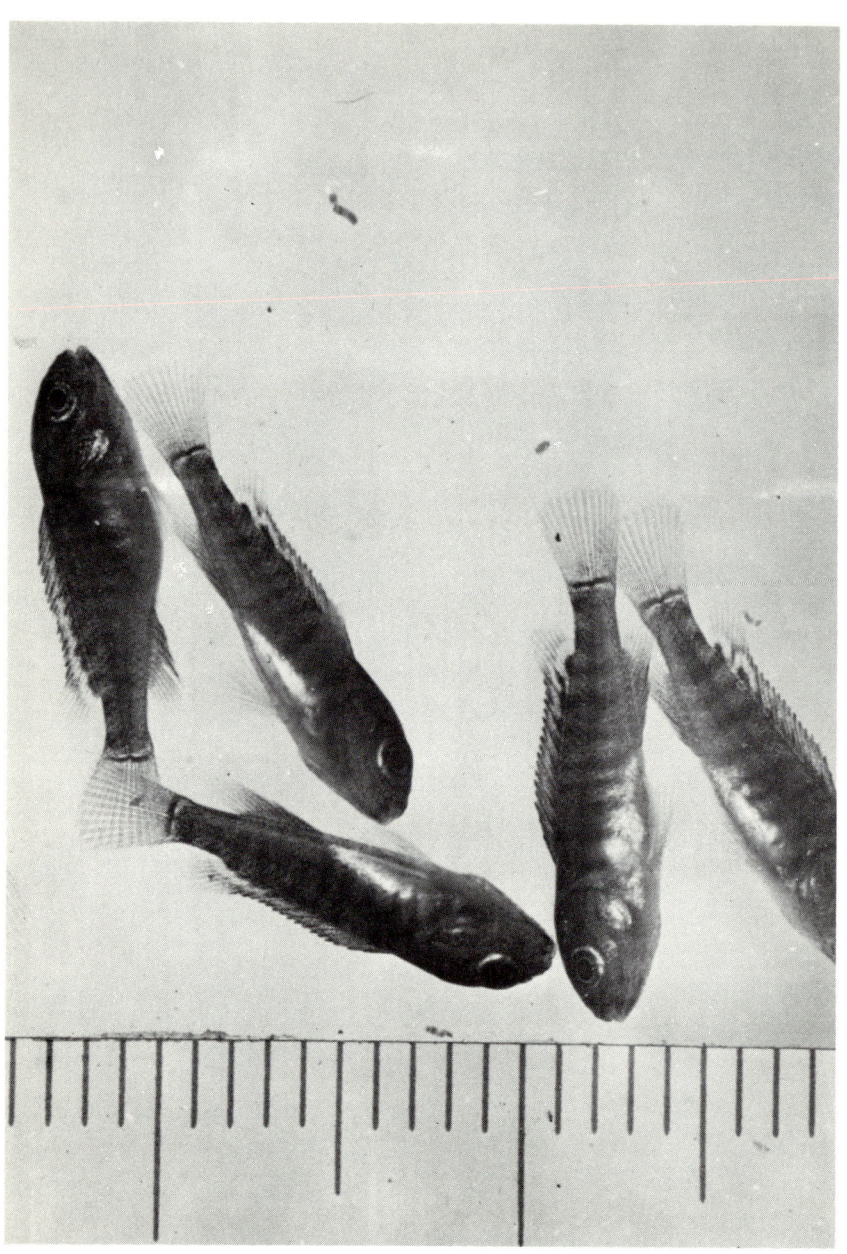

19-day old young of *L. fuelleborni* measuring about 13 mm long. During the early stages of independent life they are susceptible to a fungus disease. Photo by Dr. D. Terver.

Labeotropheus fuelleborni is known only from Lake Malawi and was named in honor of Dr. Fuelleborn, a sergeant in the German army and surveyor of Lake Malawi, by Dr. Ahl. Photo by Dr. D. Terver.

Except for the much stouter body of a ripe female both the male and female *Hyphessobrycon griemi* look alike. Photo by Ruda Zukal.

Breeding Griem's Tetra
Hyphessobrycon griemi

In 1956 Harald Schultz went on an expedition into the Goias area of Brazil. In writing to me he mentioned that he had found *Hyphessobrycon flammeus,* similar to those which Dr. George Myers found near Rio de Janeiro, differing only in that they quickly faded as soon as they were captured. It was a pity for they were such lovely fish.

A good plant cover is needed in spawning *Hyphessobrycon griemi* as in many tetras but enough open space should be left for the pre-spawning activities shown in these photographs by R. Zukal.

The wild form of *H. griemi (?)* from Rio, the shoulder markings contrasting strongly against the delicate reddish blush of the body and fins. They are also relatively small measuring less than 1½ inches long. Photo by Dr. H. R. Axelrod.

These washed out Tetra from Rio's became a new species when Hoedemann, the famous Dutch scientist, took the trouble to study preserved specimens, and he named it *Hyphessobrycon griemi* in honor of Walter Griem of Aquarium Hamburg, Hamburg, Germany. Even though Griem's Tetra and the Tetra from Rio look very much alike when both are in excellent condition, they have very different characteristics. *Hyphessobrycon griemi* is a much more sensitive and less colorful fish and were it not for Rudi Zukal finding a few specimens in Czechoslovakia, bringing them to their peak of condition and recording their spawning in beautiful color pictures, as well as black and whites, the aquarium world might have lost interest in this beautiful fish.

The color photographs show some of the color phases of *Hyphessobrycon griemi*. At times they show their two shoulder stripes very plainly, while at other times they are almost invisible. Their basic color changes, too, from a deep red, to a rosy pink, to an almost olive drab. Hopefully someone with a great deal of experience studying the physical

These *H. griemi* individuals are apparently starved or sick. The caudal fin of the fish at the left is also partly damaged. Photo by R. Zukal.

Male and female *H. griemi,* bodies almost parallel moving towards the bottom and below, the male moving closer to the stouter bellied female on the right a few moments prior to spawning. Photos by R. Zukal.

The spawning pair leaves the spawning site and below, starting all over again this time close to the surface of the water. Photos by R. Zukal.

characteristics of these small tetras (like Dr. Jacques Gery, George Myers or Stan Weitzman) should compare large series of *Hyphessobrycon griemi, bifasciatus* and *flammeus.* They must be closely related because all of them change color very readily, very rapidly and very distinctly.

Since the Griem Tetra rarely exceeds $1\frac{1}{4}$ inches in total length, it is a small tetra and as such requires rather small foods. To condition them properly they must have the finest foods. Freeze-dried tubifex worms, brine shrimp and freeze-dried flake foods are extremely good foods, but some live foods such as newly hatched brine shrimp, live *Daphnia* or

The female *H. griemi* (lower fish) is obviously ready to drop her eggs. Free spawners produce great numbers of eggs but the parents are also notorious for eating their own eggs. Photo by Dr. S. Frank.

A male *H. griemi* displaying in front of the female. The shoulder spots are indicated in both fishes. Photo by R. Zukal.

very clean live tubifex worms must be included in their diets if they are to be brought to the peak of breeding condition.

This tetra can tolerate water as low in temperature as 65°F., but it is not recommended. A well planted aquarium, small in size, say, below five gallons, with an open area in the center, is ideal for spawning Griem's Tetra. The water should be soft and acid, darkened, preferably, with peat moss extract. The temperature should be about 72° and it should be slowly raised to 77° after the pair have been in the tank together for 30 minutes.

A spawning pair of *H. griemi* in action, their bodies still wrapped about each other; the eggs slowly float away and below, the eggs slowly drop towards the bottom as the pair breaks violently apart with the tail of the female out of the water. Photos by R. Zukal.

While the sex differences in many tetras are fairly easy to distinguish by the male's usually longer fins, this is not true with Griem's Tetra. Both male and female have almost identical fin characteristics and about the only true way to sex live fish is to wait for the females to fatten up with spawn. When the female's bellies become distended with roe, the slim males are easily recognized and the sexes should immediately be separated.

Spawning is such a violent affair that the tiny eggs are hurled a good distance from the spawning pair shown here. Photo by R. Zukal.

Breeding in nature (Brazil for this species) takes place only during the rainy season when the banks of the river overflow and the fishes can eat a more nourishing diet. The spawning in nature is done in clumps of grass on the flooded grasslands and the fry have many places to hide in the flooded savannahs until they grow strong enough to flee from attackers. In the aquarium there is no problem or feeding or fresh water, so Griem's Tetra spawns all year and it is quite possible to spawn a pair every month, with two hundred fry being raised at each spawning. Assuming you have introduced a well-conditioned pair of Griem's Tetras to their small, well-planted aquarium, you can expect them to spawn as soon as the temperature reaches 77°F.

To begin, the male does the usual exotic dance in front of his fair lady. He seems to be in great spirits and if you use water which has been recently taken directly from the tap and well aerated for two days, you'll probably have a very active and very colorful male as they like "fresh" water. The colors of both fish heighten as the dance goes on and the stripes on the sides gradually disappear. Soon the female begins following the male and in a few hours, or as much as 48 hours, the female will follow the male into the thickets. Almost as soon as they reach the first bunch of plants, the male pushes his body against the female, while lined up almost parallel to her, and the eggs begin to fly. At every "squeeze" about 10-60 eggs are released. At best the pair ignore the eggs, though at times they may eat a few.

As soon as the real spawning begins to take place, the male seems to become more and more aggressive and he bites the fins of the female. This biting is also observed during the pre-spawning ritual, and aside from a few torn fins there is no real harm done. The fighting is nothing like *Betta splendens* spawning activity in terms of damage and I've never lost any of the *H. griemi* we spawned due to fighting.

As spawning continues over about 130 minutes in total, the male forces the female to release her eggs in almost every corner of the aquarium.

Depending upon the temperature, the young may hatch in from one to three days and the usual amount of fry that are raised is about 200, regardless of the number of eggs laid.

Fry raised under ideal conditions are ready to spawn themselves in eight months, which, in Brazil, means that they are ready to spawn at the beginning of the next rainy season in which they were themselves spawned.

Hyphessobrycon griemi is an ideal fish for every community aquarium. It is very peaceful and when happy and well cared for, it has a most attractive red coloration.

The Blue Convict Cichlid
Cichlasoma spilurum

Even the experts can make mistakes, and so much has been written about this fish that contradicted my own experience that I studied the fish a bit further and found that what everyone thought was the convict cichlid, *Cichlasoma nigrofasciatum*, was, in many cases, *Cichlasoma spilurum*. This is interesting because *C. nigrofasciatum* is a cave spawner and produces quite a group of eggs inside a flowerpot or other deep, dark secret cave, while *spilurum*

The male fish at the background lacks the dark spot on the dorsal fin characteristic of the female *Cichlasoma spilurum*. Photo by R. Zukal.

A few eggs laid earlier by the female are seen attached to the surface of a large piece of rock; below, the male much larger in size almost completely hiding the spawning female from view. Photos by R. Zukal.

The male waiting for the upside-down female to finish laying a few more eggs and below, the male fertilizing the eggs as the female temporarily rests. Photos by R. Zukal.

A male *C. spilurum* is usually larger, its fins longer and body deeper than those of the female. Photo by R. Zukal.

The convict cichlid, *Cichlasoma nigrofasciatum* is a species often confused with the blue convict. Photo by Dr. R. J. Goldstein.

It is once more the female's turn to spawn. The eggs are attached at random but not touching each other. Photo by R. Zukal.

The female is reluctant to leave the spawning site, eagerly anxious for the male to withdraw.
Photo by R. Zukal.

The female occasionally strays a short distance away from the spawning site but, below, invariably returns to continue adding more eggs. Photos by R. Zukal.

Highly territorial, especially while guarding the nest, these cichlids are ready to confront and challenge all intruders. Photo by J. Kassanyi.

wouldn't be caught dead in a cave. For them, the more open their nest is, the better they like it. So, should you wonder whether you have the right convict cichlid, you can be fairly certain that if they look like a grey, striped cichlid (see photos accompanying this article) and they spawn in caves, they are *C. nigrofasciatum*. If they spawn out in the open, they are *C. spilurum*. I wonder what would be the spawning habit of a cross between the two?

The male *spilurum* is the larger of the pair and, as he gets older, a pronounced bump forms on his head which scientists call "frontal gibbosity." His dorsal and anal fins are also more pointed and longer than the female's. The female, though smaller than the male, can take good care of herself during the pre-spawning ritual.

Under normal circumstances all it takes to spawn this fish is a pair, live food, and an aquarium. I have used 10 gallon aquaria very successfully. Usually I leave chunks of slate (broken aquarium bottom slates serve perfectly) lying at odd angles in the tank. The pair, after going through the usual dancing mouth-to-mouth wrestling and tail beating, start nipping the spawning site. After they are satisfied with its cleanliness and the male has worked himself into being a fit father, the female's ovipositor protrudes a bit and she begins her egg-laying. I have had this fish spawn on the bottom of the tank, the glass sides of the tank, a heater tube, a plastic filter stem and on rocks. I have never had them show any interest in a cave or in a flowerpot. For commercial purposes I remove the slate and hatch the eggs artificially, but the *spilurum* are good parents and they usually eat only a few of their babies.

Unless these fish are fed heavily with live foods, especially live, fresh *Tubifex* worms, they will not attain spawning

A dozen more eggs and the spawning is over. Photo by R. Zukal.

Not all the eggs of *C. spilurum* shown here are expected to develop. The few eggs that appear dull, white and opaque are already dead. Photo by R. Zukal.

condition. Also, by maintaining the breeders separately, they will spawn within a few days of being put together in the same aquarium.

The young hatch in from two to three days and once they become free-swimming, they will eagerly take newly hatched brine shrimp. The fry and breeders are very hardy.

Most cichlids like slightly alkaline, hard water, especially the American cichlids (from Central and South America). I use a mineral water with a pH of 7.9 and quite hard. They will probably spawn in any kind of water.

These are very interesting, mild-manner cichlids, very suitable for the beginner. They are extremely hardy and, except for their reliance on live foods, are very easy to keep. Try a few pair the next time you see them . . . but offer them caves, too, since you never know which convict cichlid you are really getting until you spawn them!

(Above). The male attacks the female by prodding her towards the thickets. (Below) The female, ready for spawning, leads the male into the soft plants where she will spawn. Photos by R. Zukal.

The Black Tetra

Gymnocorymbus ternetzi

What tetra spawns just as easily in almost any kind of water, is very popular with millions being sold every year, has almost no color except black and white, eats everything live or frozen, and is very hardy?

If you said the black tetra you were right and why this fish is so popular is quite beyond my understanding . . . until

A pair of black tetras; the male is smaller than the female and more intensely colored black. Photo by Ruda Zukal.

The Czechs and Poles first developed the long-finned black tetra, now popularly known as G.T.O. (from **Gymnocorymbus ternetzi**... OH!) The author brought back spawning pairs and introduced them into the free world. Photos above and on the facing page by Dr. Herbert R. Axelrod.

As the pair approach the thickets they align themselves (above). As they release their eggs and sperm, they droop their dorsal fins about one another. Photos by Ruda Zukal.

Spawning continues as the pair push violently against each other (above). They continually flex their bodies as the sexual products are shed. Photos by Ruda Zukal.

Not all spawnings are successful. It seems, without extensive verification that only males which are very dark will spawn successfully with females which are faded and pale. The fish, both of them, should always be active and well fed prior to their introduction to the spawning aquarium. Photos by Ruda Zukal.

In all successful spawnings the pair align themselves next to each other and, in a close, side-by-side position, wriggle their way through the vegetation shedding eggs and sperm as they go. For this reason fine-leaved plants which are soft enough for the pair to penetrate should be used in the spawning tank. Photos by Ruda Zukal.

A healthy male, the lowest fish, with two females. The upper female is not ready for spawning, but the lower female is full, plump and ready to spawn. Photo by G. J. M. Timmerman.

Black tetras spawn violently, flexing themselves against each other to help shed the sperm and eggs. Photos by Ruda Zukal.

Prior to reaching spawning condition, the long-finned black tetras have already developed their beautiful finnage. On the facing page the much darker male and the larger female have reached spawning size. Photos by Dr. Herbert R. Axelrod.

Francisek Kawalec, in Poland, produced the G.T.O., the long-finned black tetra, in 1964. I brought the first specimens from Czechoslovakia in 1966 and they were introduced to the American public a few months later in early 1967. The original stock spawned about 80% true and the longer-finned G.T.O.s were constantly inbred to each other until finally, in 1969 almost 100% true strains were available.

Breeding all black tetras, both long-finned and normals, is the same process. You can even cross the long-finned G.T.O.s with the normal variety and, if the normal fish used were offspring of G.T.O.s, then you'll get about 25% G.T.O.s

After spawning is completed (above) the female leaves the spawning site (below) but the male chases her, even at the surface of the water (facing page). Black tetras should be spawned in a covered aquarium as they frequently jump out of the aquarium in their excitement. Photos by Ruda Zukal.

To be ready for spawning is the whole key to success. Keep male and female fish in separate aquaria. When the heavy females begin to bulge with spawn they may be matched with active males in an aquarium of about 5 gallon capacity. The tank should be completely filled with artificial spawning grass so the entire bottom and the first 25% of the tank's depth is completely clogged. Of course you can use fine-leaved plants like *Myriophyllum* or *Caboma* if you wish, but the use of live plants always is accompanied with the danger of introducing unwanted parasites.

Place the fish in pairs, or two males to each female, into the spawning tank. Use water which is soft and slightly acid, though almost any kind of water which supports life is acceptable. I have spawned black tetras in water with pH ranges from 5·6 to 8·4 and from soft to hard. The temperature need not be high for black tetras are almost temperate

On the facing page is a typical, inbred female black tetra which won a prize in Germany. Above are examples of the first long-finned black tetras which the author brought back from Czechoslovakia. Photos by Dr. Herbert R. Axelrod.

During this spawning sequence the female jumped out of the water! Photos by Ruda Zukal.

fish. If you maintain the fish at about 70°, raise the temperature in the spawning tank after you've introduced the fish, to 78°. Spawning takes place quickly, usually within 48 hours. Keep your eye on the breeders as once they have completed spawning, or even during spawning, they will egghunt and eat as many eggs as they can find. The reason for the dense planting is to hide the eggs from the breeders.

The fry hatch in a few days and must be fed infusoria for a day or two and then newly hatched brine shrimp. The adults can be conditioned on freeze-dried brine shrimp or freeze-dried *Tubifex* worms. They also accept all the usual flakefood fare, but some live food is always welcome and necessary to bring the breeders to their peak of condition.

In commercial operations a few dozen aquaria are set up at the same time and all the spawns are raised in one large tank. Males are usually smaller than females, but the females are so much more plump than males that sexing them is not too much of a problem. The G.T.O. males seem to have longer finnage than females, but this is not too reliable as a differentiating sexual characteristic.

The fish on the right has the characteristic lump on the head found among the males of the Sierra Leone Cichlid. Photo by E. Roloff.

The Sierra Leone Cichlid

Pelmatochromis thomasi

Mr. E. Roloff is a banker in Germany who has been fascinated by fishes for many years. Every year he spends his vacation in another part of the world bringing back mostly killifishes, small tetras and dwarf cichlids. In 1962, while searching for more interesting annual fishes, Roloff stumbled upon this dwarf cichlid, which was eventually identified as *Pelmatochromis thomasi*. This name will probably be changed as soon as the revision of the genus *Pelmatochromis* is completed.

A young male *Pelmatochromis thomasi*. The lump on the head may not be very distinct yet but note his longer pelvic fins. Photo by H. Hansen.

Adult female Sierra Leone Cichlid. Photo by Dr. S. Frank.

The features of the male (left) and female *P. thomasi* are shown clearly in this photograph by E. Roloff.

In most respects this fish, though African in origin, looks and acts like the typical small *Aequidens* species from South America with which we are so familiar. As with *Aequidens*, there is not too much difference between the sexes and the best sexual difference I can find is the shape of the head. The female has a rounded, smooth profile to her head, while the male has a distinct lump on his head. This is clear when you study the accompanying photos, especially the photo taken by Mr. Roloff of the original pair of fish.

Spawning the Sierra Leone cichlid is easy. Condition the breeders on the best foods available. Live foods are preferable (this is true of almost all situations), but freeze-dried and frozen foods are also acceptable. The sexes should have been kept separated and, as soon as the female begins to get a distinct plump appearance, you should prepare a spawning tank. The usual dwarf cichlid spawning tank with its flat rocks and subdued lighting is all that is necessary.

Pre-spawning activities of *P. thomasi* looking over a possible spawning site and below, hovering and displaying above the selected site. Photos by R. Zukal.

A female *P. thomasi* starting to spawn on top of a flat clean substrate as the male waits for his turn.

The male shedding his milt starting from the left edge of the egg nest.

Fertilizing the more centrally located eggs.

A few more drops of milt on the periphery of the nest.

With the ovipositor extended the female attaches a few more eggs.

The male waiting patiently for his turn once more. Photos by H. J. Richter.

As the fish perform the typical tail-beating, displaying, mouth locking formalities, they quickly get down to the business of nipping a rock until it is clean enough upon which to deposit their spawn.

These fish are not very aggressive and the male rarely bullies the female. They do have one single peculiarity though, and that is the main difference between them and *Aequidens*. It is very frequent, almost always, that *Hemichromis* and *Aequidens*, when they spawn, will, at some time during the spawning act, swim in circles over the spawning site in a head to tail parade. The female, laying her eggs

With the pelvic fins touching the substrate a male *P. thomasi* fertilizes the eggs accompanied by slight tremors of the body. Photos by R. Zukal.

Like a string of pearls the eggs are attached carefully one at a time. Photo by R. Zukal.

as she slowly circles the spawning site, the male fertilizing as he follows her. None of the observers of this fish have ever seen the pair spawning simultaneously. Usually the female lays her eggs while the male hovers closely by; as soon as she leaves the spawning site, he descends to fertilize the eggs. When he is finished and leaves the spawning site, she returns. This is an interesting variation in fish behavior and ethologists should attempt to discover the significance of this, if any.

Unfortunately, I have never been successful in raising the young of this species as they almost always have eaten the eggs, but I assume the eggs would hatch in a few days and the young would thrive on the usual fare of infusoria and freshly hatched brine shrimp.

The bluish iridescent cast on the body is the predominant feature of the wild form of *Brachydanio albolineatus*. Photo by Dr. S. Frank.

The Pearl Danio

Brachydanio albolineatus

From the clear running streams of Sumatra, Burma and remote parts of Thailand, comes a tiny fish with long barbels that never stops swimming and poking about the middle reaches of the waters. The pearl danio, one of the "beginners' fish," has been known to science since 1860 and has been available to aquarists since the early 1920's. Why it isn't much more popular is hard to understand as the fish is hardy, eats all kinds of dried, frozen, freeze-dried and live foods and rarely succumbs to disease.

Sexing the pearl danio is very simple since the males are always very slender, while the females, even when not bulging with eggs, are much fuller than the males.

Two varieties of pearl danio are known. The blue strain is the normal fish found in the wild, while the golden red

The golden red variety of pearl danio was the result of inbreeding, however the blue color of the wild form is still evident. Photo by Dr. Herbert R. Axelrod.

The female *B. albolineatus* is following the male towards the planted area of the tank. Photos by R. Zukal.

Amorous nipping accompanies courtship and below, the body curved like an *S*, the male begins to wrap his tail around the body of the female a few moments before spawning. Photos by R. Zukal.

Free-spawning pearl danios produce many eggs which may be eaten as soon as they are laid. However, this danger can be minimized by procedures discussed in the text. Photo by R. Zukal.

strain is the result of careful inbreeding by German aquarists during the 1930's. The gold strain is much easier to breed and maintain than the wild form.

Like its close relative, *Brachydanio rerio*, the zebra danio, the pearl lays non-adhesive eggs and scatters them in their frenzied orgy of reproduction. To successfully breed the fish, the following methods have been utilized. Use a tank as long as possible. The bottom of the tank may be covered with round, glass marbles, slotted rods, $\frac{1}{4}$-inch plastic mesh or fine-leaved plants. The water above the spawning medium should be as low as practical, 2 inches being ideal. One pair of fish for every 144 square inches of bottom is an ideal ratio should you prefer to use group spawning. More success is assured with having six heavy females with ten active males.

Set up the aquarium with freshly aged water with a pH between 6.0 and 6.8; use the softest water available and keep the males and females separated from each other. Observe the females constantly for if they become too heavy with eggs, they will spawn without a male (laying infertile eggs of course).

The fish spawn in a very delightful, amorous manner with both males and females chasing each other, lining themselves up side by side, and finally, with the male wrapping his body over the top of the female, using the female's dorsal fin as a pivot; eggs are scattered in a very haphazard fashion. The breeders often turn around and gobble up the slowly falling eggs, thus the need for shallow water. In the wild, in fast-running streams, the eggs are carried away as fast as they are laid, but in the tank other means must be used. By keeping the breeders as full of food as possible, this egg-eating is kept to a minimum.

With the previously laid eggs still floating slowly down this pair of *B. albolineatus* are already on their way to spawning again. Photo by R. Zukal.

Their bodies coiled about each other the eggs are hurled violently. A few of them get caught in the foliage and the rest eventually reach the bottom of the tank. Below, the still swollen body of the female pearl danio on the left indicates that more spawnings can be expected. Photos by R. Zukal.

Side view of a spawning pair of *B. albolineatus*. Note the fine, long barbels of this species and below, both fish busy eating the eggs they just shed. It is now time to remove them before all the eggs are consumed. Photos by R. Zukal.

Remove the breeders after assuring yourself that they have spawned. I use glass-bottomed tanks and shine a strong light up through the bottom, thus highlighting the eggs. When many eggs are seen, I remove the breeders and raise the young in the spawning tank.

The large eggs take about 36 hours to hatch at 82° F., which is an ideal spawning temperature, though the fish should be maintained in aquaria with a temperature around 75° F. It takes almost a week before the fry are able to swim freely and absorb their huge yolk sacs. Once they are free swimming they can easily be raised on egg infusion or infusoria. Newly hatched brine shrimp is also accepted.

The slender body of the male in contrast to the much deeper female on the left precludes confusing the sexes in *B. albolineatus.* The females of this species are aggressive spawners! Photo by Ruda Zukal.

Healthy five-banded barbs are active, very iridescent and with rosy tints on their fins. The female has a deeper body. Photo by Dr. S. Frank.

Five-Banded Barb

Barbodes pentazona Boulenger

This beautifully patterned and delicately colored fish belongs to a group of banded fishes of the very large group of barbs of the family Cyprinidae, the carp-like fishes. The well-known tiger barb *(Puntius tetrazona)* with four bands is considered by systematists as the original form from which the five-banded *(B. pentazona)*, six-banded *(B. hexagona)*, and the interrupted banded *(Capoeta partipentazona)* barbs presumably have evolved. Five-banded barbs are not common even in their natural range (Singapore, Malay Peninsula, Borneo) and are seldom seen in tropical fish shops in large numbers.

The interrupted bar distinguishes *partipentazona* from other species of banded barbs with complete bands. Photo by G. J. M. Timmerman.

In temperament they are more peaceful and in appearance just as good-looking but not as prolific as the tigers. In addition this species is not as sensitive to water conditions as *P. tetrazona* which succumbs easily to foul water conditions.

The silvery body is yellowish and with 5 bluish black bands across the body. Healthy individuals have pink to reddish tints on their abdomens and fins. The females are easily distinguished from the males by their larger size, deeper bodies and lighter color. The black bands of the males are sharper and the red cast more intense especially at breeding time.

In general barbs are active fishes and require rather large aquaria with well-aerated water. They thrive well in soft, slightly acid water with a temperature between 74° to 84°F. Moderate amount of vegetation, including some floating types, should provide these fish protection from each other and from strong light. They accept all types of food; they are so greedy in fact that they should be fed often, but in reasonable amounts only. They also eat detritus, algae and uneaten food on the bottom.

Prior to spawning the selected parents must be conditioned with live food and kept apart from each other for a few days. It is known that those fish which have previously paired in the community tank also become better spawners. A 5-gallon tank will serve as a spawning tank but the temperature should be raised about 5°F. above that to which they have become accustomed. Fine leafy plants are needed, not only to provide some protection to the female, but to catch the eggs scattered during mating. However, they should not be too dense to smother the fishes.

The spawning process in *B. pentazona* is typical for barbs. However, in comparison to the very prolific tiger barbs they are less willing to mate and produce fewer eggs. As soon as an apparently compatible pair is chosen courtship could follow. The male will display and approach the female and persist in chasing her although not violently enough to cause injury. She seemingly chooses the spawning spot and as she pauses the male snuggles to her side, their bodies parallel and his tail coiled about her posterior end.

Notice the complete dorsal band characteristic of the six-banded barb. Photo by Milan Chvojka.

The tiger barb also known as the four-banded barb is a colorful fish and easy to keep. They have been bred in great numbers commercially. Photo by H. Hansen.

The body color of the six-banded barb (photo by Dr. H. R. Axelrod) is usually paler than the more rosy banded barb below in the photo by Dr. S. Frank.

The male five-banded barb chases the female persistently from the rear and below, she pauses meanwhile investigating a possible spawning site. Photos by R. Zukal.

As the female slows down the male makes a quick move to get into the side-by-side stance below. Photos by R. Zukal.

A large belly and a slightly protruding genital region are reliable indicators of the ripeness of a female. Below, a ripe female shows her interest in spawning by actively leading the male to selected sites. Photos by R. Zukal.

Within seconds the eggs are extruded a few at a time; he fertilizes them immediately. This is accompanied by much trembling. The eggs are scattered and, being only slightly adhesive, simply cling to the plants or fall to the bottom. Spawning is repeated several times with the female looking for new spots at random with the intervals between active spawning progressively getting longer.

Barbs are well known for eating their eggs and young but during the early stages of sexual excitation they are too preoccupied to eat. Later they will actively hunt the eggs to eat. As soon as this occurs they should be removed. Between 100 to 200 eggs are produced. These hatch into small, delicate fry after 2 to 3 days depending on the temperature. The fry are attached to the undersurface of the leaves and sides of the tank for about six days or until the

Once encouraged the male persists keeping his position even as the female dives almost vertically to the bottom. Photo by R. Zukal.

During the height of spawning frenzy these banded barbs can spawn on top of the bare substrate or below, in a clump of vegetation. Photos by R. Zukal.

For greater support during spawning the male wraps his tail tightly behind the dorsal fin of the female. Photos by R. Zukal.

Preparing to spawn in the midst of a feathery plant bush which can minimize egg predation by these notorious egg eaters. Photos by R. Zukal.

With good care and feeding this pair will be ready to breed again in about six weeks. Photo by R. Zukal.

yolk sac is completely absorbed. By this time they swim freely and are able to accept small live food like infusorians and very fine powdered dried food. They should be fed newly hatched brine shrimp immediately after their mouths are large enough to ingest them. Larger live food as *Daphnia* and *Cyclops* could overpower these delicate young and should be offered only much later. Uniform temperature is also critical during this period. Sudden temperature change easily could wipe out an entire brood.

The young grow fast and within a couple of weeks the color and body bands are evident. They should be sorted according to size and placed in larger containers preferably by themselves or with other similar sized species. Within a year they are sexually mature and can be bred every six weeks in captivity if properly fed and maintained.

A close view of the iridescent spots on the gill area of the jewel cichlid. Photo by J. Kassanyi.

The Jewel Cichlid
Hemichromis bimaculatus II

by Dr. Herbert R. Axelrod

Regardless of what you may think, this is probably the most colorful freshwater fish in the whole, wide world. The cardinal tetra may have more blue and be more attractive in its tiny splendor, but its color intensity, variation and percentage of body coverage falls far below this new variety known in Europe as *Hemichromis bimaculatus* II. The "II" signifies it is merely a second color variety.

There is a vast amount of published information about this fish because its colors, breeding habits and physiology have been the bases for many studies in universities and institutes all over the world. Inspired by the extraordinary

Highly territorial, especially while guarding the nest, these jewel cichlids are ready to confront and challenge all intruders. Photo by J. Kassanyi.

A pair of the more colorful strain of *Hemichromis bimaculatus* in various phases of spawning. The red-orange colored fish is the female and the larger and dark red fish is the male. Photos by H. J. Richter.

photographs of Hans Joachim Richter, I have attempted to gather a brief sample of this information from many widespread sources and present it in as elementary a fashion as possible.

The principal color of the jewel cichlid is red. Under breeding conditions, the female is always a bright orange red, while the male is a darker violet red. These colors are based upon the erythrophores. When the fish are in non-breeding condition, they have a brownish color of distinct greenish hue. It takes several days for the erythrophores (red pigment cells) to show their effect and to change the coloration from the brown to the bright reds and oranges. Color changes within the red ranges, that is from red to orange or from orange to red, take place quickly, sometimes in a matter of minutes. The probable reason for the varying time changes is that to be red the fish must manufacture the red pigment cells (erythrophores) while in changing from red to orange it must merely suppress the black pigment cells (melanophores).

A pair of jewel fish engaged in a pre-spawning test of strength. If compatible they remain faithful to each other. Photo by J. Kassanyi.

An important pre-spawning activity of substrate brooders as *H. bimaculatus* is cleaning the selected spawning site meticulously. Photos by R. Zukal.

With the fins almost touching the bottom a few more eggs are added to the site. Note the opercular spot or false eye. Photo by H. J. Richter.

A series of alternate spawnings by the male and female results in the production of a considerably large nest of eggs. Photos by H. J. Richter.

Occasionally an odd place can be considered as a spawning site in spite of the inconvenience. Photo by J. Kassanyi.

Eggs are laid down on the flat substrate with the aid of the ovipositor. Eggs are aligned almost like a string of pearls. Photo by J. Kassanyi.

There are, of course, many individual differences in color brightness and in the fish used for illustrating the breeding sequence the brightness of color was inbred, thus earning it the nickname "II" to designate it as a color variety. This designation is not a scientific designation but one used by aquarists to differentiate between the normally colored fish and the inbred, highly colored variety. There is probably not a *Hemichromis bimaculatus* II existing in the wild.

The sides of mature jewel fish are covered with from six to eight rows of green spots, pigmented with a guanin material. These pigmented cells are called guanocytes. These same spots may cover the head and fins. The eye color varies from red to yellowish green and a band through the eye becomes obvious when the fish is sexually mature.

Behind the eye on the operculum (gill cover) is an intense black patch, outlined by a yellow-green ring. The patch is not perfectly round but is oval in shape so that when the fish extends its gill covers in a menacing pose, the patch

A female jewel fish guarding the nest, a chore she shares with the male. Photo by H. J. Richter.

forms a large eyespot. Obviously, when a fish sees two big, bright eyes so far apart it becomes frightened by a fish that appears much larger than it really is.

Another kidney shaped patch appears on the side and again, should another fish see the real eye and the eye spot on the side, especially on the spawning female, they might envision a larger fish and these are the two eyes. A third spot on the base of the tail fin completely disappears when the fish begin to spawn.

The tail of the fish is very variable. By closely studying the color photographs you might ascertain as I have that the top half of the tail bears, more or less, the same color pattern as the dorsal fin, while the lower part of the tail mimics the anal fin.

Jewel fish have a definite social order and go through elaborate ceremony during breeding, fighting, boundary protection and courting. While in certain cichlids (*Tilapia*, for example) only the males become dominant in a society, female jewel fish have been known to stake out a territory

The male is aerating the eggs by moving the pectorals rapidly. Photo by H. J. Richter.

The male ejecting milt over the eggs. During the process his body color is intensified. Photo by J. Kassanyi.

and to vigorously defend their territory against invaders. Territorial claims are closely tied in with reproduction and, should an active, sexually aroused male be removed from the aquarium, several other non-sexually stimulated males will fight for this vacated place and the one who succeeds usually becomes colored in a sexually-stimulated manner. The owners of a territory almost always remain near the bottom, where spawning will take place, and he (or she) rarely will chase a fish from the surface of the water, over their territory, if the invading, trespassing fish is not in sexually stimulated color.

The formation of pairs in the jewel fish has been well documented. Only in very large tanks can you keep unpaired females together with males. These females will never voluntarily enter the territory of the male. In order to study what happens when an unpaired female enters the realm of a male, it was necessary to actually use a tank divider and fence the female in so she could not escape from the male's territory. As soon as the female crosses the boundary of the territory, the male erects his median fins and takes on a brighter color almost immediately. He moves towards the female with fins erected to the utmost, showing his side in brilliant dances. This same threatening pose is shown to an aggressive male. After swimming around the female and doing a bit of tail-beating, he attacks her with a swift forward rush and butts her. This would start a battle if the fish

The male shown here ready to move in as soon as the female finishes laying a few more eggs. The female coloration never reaches the intensity of the male's. Photo by J. Kassanyi.

The bright red color, the iridescent body, the dark spots and menacing attitude all serve as visual signals to other fishes to keep away from this jewel fish guarding the nest of eggs. Photo by H. J. Richter.

was a male. If the fish is a ripe, eager female, with fully developed ovaries showing an ovipositor, she will go through the identical actions of the male, but without the vicious nature of the butts. The ripe female will not run from the male but will tolerate his attacks with just a slight budge to offset the pain of his attacks.

A female not ready for spawning will do everything in her power to get away from the male, even crashing repeatedly against the glass imprisoning her in the male's territory.

In all cases the fish move about the territory, sometimes the male following the female, othertimes the female following the male. With the ripe female, the butting and attacking gradually diminish but with certain males, especially those which haven't had a female for an extended period of time (six months or more), they become so vicious they may kill. I have successfully employed another male, or even a mirror, so the male would have his fighting efforts diluted. After a short period of time I always removed the second male and the mirror so the pair could carry on with their spawning.

Finally, after a few hours, the male accepts the female for his mate, and he signifies his acceptance of his mate by head-jerking and quivering. The final "I do" is signified by the male taking a mouthful of sand and spitting it. This digging is typical of almost all American cichlids as well. Digging is not always observed with the jewel fish.

The behaviour of the fish is entertaining at this point. The butting actually becomes part of the spawning ritual. The male will butt the female gently, whereupon the female quivers and shakes in "ecstasy". The male seems to derive a great deal of satisfaction from this and he will swim away from the female and fake a vicious rush at her, gently butt her and wait for her shakes and quivers. Often the male will rush the female but not butt her. Instead he might attack a plant or a rock and it is my belief that he is merely stalling for time until he produces the sperm necessary to fulfill his marital contract.

The quivering, shaking motions which are initially carried out in all parts of the territory, gradually center upon the selected spawning site. In some cases the male selects the site first; in other cases the female selects the site, but as the quivering progresses it becomes localized at what will eventually be the spawning site. Soon, the first fish will attack the surface with its mouth, after first having fanned the surface to remove as much loose detritus as possible. As the pair attack the surface with their mouths, they gradually stop the shivering and shaking. They do not rest until the surface is very clean. As soon as the mouthing stops (this mouthing is sometimes called "nipping" by fish ethologists), the fish go through the "dry runs." A dry run is, by definition, a false spawning where the female presses her abdomen against the spawning site, going through all the motions of laying eggs . . . except there are no eggs! The behaviorists call this "skimming" and they point out in many animals how skimming is such an important part of sex play.

Depending upon the female, skimming may end in a few moments or last for hours, but as soon as the female lays her first row of eggs, the male will fertilize them.

I have often seen males that almost completely ignored females in their territory until the female laid her first row of eggs, at which time he quickly swam over and fertilized them.

The closeup color photography of Richter shows the egg-laying process magnificently. The eggs are laid close to each other, even touching each other, but not on top of one another. They are laid in spurts of about ten eggs at a time, first in straight lines, then the lines begin to form a crude circle (see the photographs).

The male initially fertilizes the eggs every time a string is laid by the female, but, once the eggs begin to cover the spawning site, he does not always find the eggs that the female has just lain, so he fertilizes almost at random. His sperm seem active for the eggs are always 99% fertilized.

The fry with the yolk almost gone swim close to the parents like a herd of sheep. Photo by H. J. Richter.

During spawning, minor nipping might continue by the partner not involved in the reproductive act, but once spawning is completed, the pair engage solely in digging. All other activities like jerking, quivering, nipping off, skimming, tail fluttering and exaggerated brake swimming beats, are suspended.

Until spawning commences there is no question that the male is the superior social animal, but once the eggs have been laid, the female becomes very aggressive and may chase the male out of the center of his own territory so that he seems permanently stationed at the boundary of the territory policing it against intruders.

The laying of eggs has been recorded at all times of the day and night. There has never been a positive correlation between amount of light, angle of light or time of day as far as egglaying is concerned. Certainly I have never known these fish to lay their eggs in the dark, nor have I observed spawning at sunrise or sunset. The average spawning time has always been, conveniently, right after lunch!

Eggs are always laid against something hard. In an aquarium the jewel fish prefers a rock or some other horizontal surface; they do not spawn on vertical surfaces unless they have no choice. They prefer a wide surface to a small surface. They prefer a round area, say 5 inches square, or 25 square inches, to $12\frac{1}{2} \times 2$ inches (25 square inches). I have never observed jewel fish laying eggs on a leaf, but I have found them in Africa having spawned in an old automobile tire. The fish seem to be color blind as far as their spawning site is concerned and I have offered tiles of many colors and there never seemed to be a preference.

When I switched from tiles to flowerpots, which are almost universally orange-red, the females always selected these flowerpots as spawning sites. Once they spawned on a red flowerpot and I offered them painted (black, white and yellow) flowerpots, they always chose the red one.

The numbers of eggs varied with the size and age of the

A close-up photo of the eggs attached to a rocky substrate. Both parents take turns fanning and cleaning the surface of the eggs. Unattended eggs would appear fuzzy and opaque after a few days. Photo by J. Kassanyi.

It is suggested that the movements of the different fins of the parent fish serve as "call" signals to the fry. Photo by J. Kassanyi.

female. The first spawning of six females averaged 53 eggs. Females that have spawned a dozen times or more lay more than 500 eggs.

The eggs and fry which are attached to the rock are constantly aerated by one of the parents. The fish swims over the eggs and moves its fins in an exaggerated motion without moving from the spot, thus causing a powerful flow of water over the eggs. In most cases the pair share in this aerating job, but in as many as 30% of the cases, the female refused to allow the male near the nest and she took care of all the housework. This is especially true in cases where the female and male are the only fish in the tank; in cases where a spawning has taken place in a community tank, both parents are kept busy chasing away the intruders and the female is much more tolerant of the male.

As the female waits for her turn to spawn again, the male moves over the eggs and sheds his milt. Note the great color difference between the male and female especially during the act of spawning. Photo by R. Zukal.

In any case, the female cares for the eggs much more than the male. The males often leave the nesting site for hours, while the female rarely leaves for more than two minutes. The female only leaves the nest when approached by the male, at which time she cautiously leaves, assuring herself that the male will indeed take over this responsibility.

Since the eggs take $2\frac{1}{2}$–3 days to hatch, the parents have quite a bit of work to do in aerating the eggs and often they can be seen nipping the eggs. The unfertilized eggs quickly lose their adhesiveness and are always removed by the mouthing action of the parents. If you hatch the eggs artificially with an airstone taking the place of the parents, you'll probably find that those eggs which become loose are infertile. Not all infertile eggs become cloudy and not all cloudy eggs are infertile. Oftentimes a fertilized egg dies and becomes covered with fungus which might kill the adjoining eggs. If the parents don't remove these eggs (they almost always do), you should remove them with a pipette or tweezers.

As the female spends long hours aerating the eggs, the male begins digging pits in various parts of his territory. The jewel fish does not, as a rule, uproot plants. He digs one or two pits. The pits are not large and deep (other cichlids dig large, deep pits) and will be used after the fry are released from their eggcases. After about 60 hours, a close look at the eggs indicates the fry moving within the eggshell. If you simply touch the eggshell with a pencil, the embryo pops out, but his yolk remains inside, thus trapping the fry for a short time. The mouthing action of the parents probably breaks most of the shells, but without the parents' help, the fry burst their own shells in due course. The parents, as they mouth the hatching eggs, suck the babies into their mouths. Carrying as few as one and as many as thirty, the breeders spit them into one of the pits. While the parents are carrying the fry in their mouths, they "chew" on them. It makes the breeder nervous but I have never seen them swallow any at this stage of the operation.

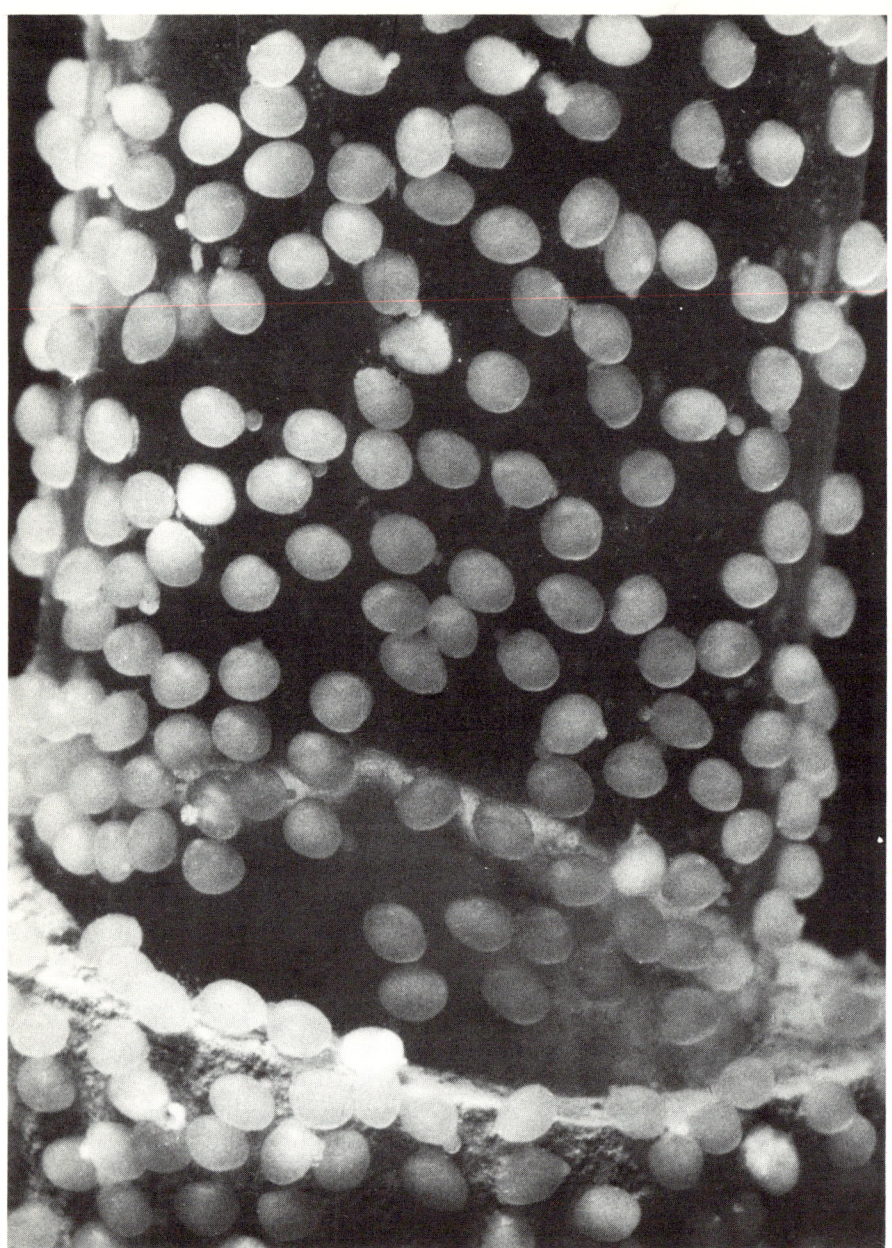
Although these eggs are situated in a rather unusual site still the fry can hatch with or without the parent's help. They are then mouthed and deposited in a shallow pit dug earlier elsewhere in the tank. Photo by J. Kassanyi.

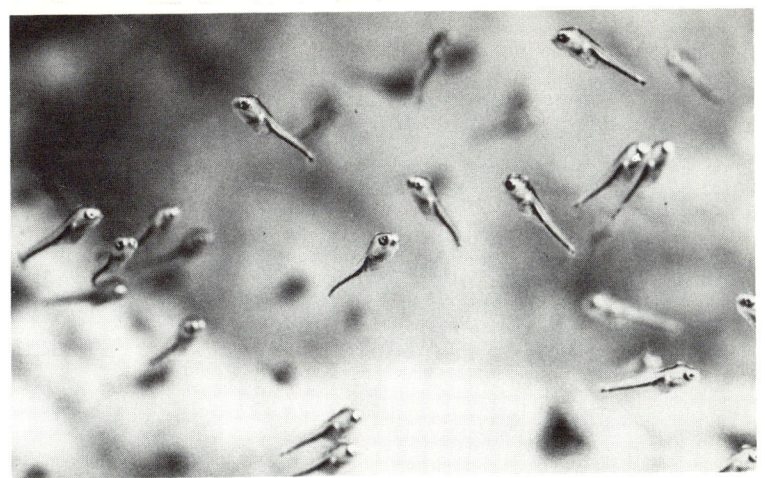

A swarm of fry already free swimming and capable of feeding on the usual fry food but still instinctively protected by the parent fish at this stage. Photo by J. Kassanyi.

Normally the parents take the young to the same pit, but not always. I have seen a male spit his mouthful of fry into one pit, while the female used another. Eventually, though, in almost all cases, the fry end up together. A close look at the action of the breeders shows that they spit the young out an inch or more above the pit. The yolk is obviously heavier than water and pulls the struggling fry down as it falls. Since the fry keeps struggling, it ends up under the yolk! There are two adhesive organs on the foremost part of the head of the fry, thus the fry attaches to the first thing it touches; usually in an aquarium this is a piece of sand. The fry keeps up the eternal tail-wagging with a beat of three to five wags per second. This wriggling, multiplied by 500 or more fry, can best be described as a quivering mass and it serves a magnificent purpose: the fish aerate themselves for they are now growing very quickly, utilizing their yolk, and the best way for them to get rid of their waste material is to fan it away . . . which is what they do. As they wriggle, their tails rise, their heads, stuck fast, cause a strong current away from the bottom. It is all very efficient.

The bright coloration of the parent *H. bimaculatus*, usually more spectacular after spawning, has been shown experimentally to keep the young in a school during the early swimming stage. Photo by H. Hansen.

After three to five days of wiggling, the yolk is absorbed and the fry becomes detached from the site of adherence and bounces its way out of the pit. Within a few hours after bouncing out of the pit, the fry can swim freely, and they form a school quite naturally.

During their first schooling experience, the fry begin to nibble and feed, eagerly taking newly hatched brine shrimp if it is available.

During life in the pit, the breeders keep aerating even though the fry create enough of their own aeration. Every so often, but with no regularity, the breeders move the mass of wriggling young to a new pit. Not every pit dug is used and sometimes when only one pit is dug, the breeders move the young to a natural cave or slight depression. Every time young try to leave the pit or school, the parents try to catch them in their mouths and spit them back into the pack. Initially the parents follow the school without trying to direct it in any way, but after a few days, the school recognizes the parents by their fiery red color, and the school follows the parents. The parents are at their highest coloration when the fry have been free swimming for a few days (see photo) and the young are so attracted to this color that they will follow a red dummy if the breeders are removed.

H. bimaculatus fry are known to follow fish dummies provided they are colored bright red as the real parent shown here. Photo by H. J. Richter.

A trio of young jewel cichlids with the markings and iridescence of the adults already evident. Photo by J. Kassanyi.

Fish, especially jewel fish, are easily fooled. The fry can be fooled by a red dummy and the breeders can be fooled by small pearls glued onto their usual flowerpot spawning site. Foster parents are even possible and I have often used *Aequidens portalegrensis* as foster parents to jewel fish. Your own experimentation in this area would be very exciting.

Should you have a very ferocious male, you might try a trick I learned quite by accident. I put a male jewel fish and a female jewel fish in a ten gallon aquarium separated by a $\frac{1}{2} \times \frac{1}{4}$ inch mesh plastic screen. The fish courted and spawned using the screen as a place to lay their eggs and the fry were successfully raised swimming from time to time from one side of the tank to the other. I would try switching the jewel fish with other fishes . . . they might even spawn with South American *Aequidens*.

Golden-Striped Rasbora

Rasbora daniconius Hamilton-Buchanan

Compared to other species of the genus *Rasbora*, *R. daniconius* is neither outstanding in its color nor its overall pattern. Yet members of this species are rather elegant in appearance, graceful in movement, peaceful in temperament and very prolific *even in captivity*. It is one of the most widely distributed members of *Rasbora* found from Thailand across Burma, Indo-China, South East India, in the Ganges Basin, Ceylon and the Greater Sunda Islands. Understandably a species of such wide distribution would exhibit some variations in color, pattern and other anatomical differences that are not obvious to the untrained eye but

Even in a black and white photo the over-all bright sheen of the body of *Rasbora daniconius* stands out in contrast to the single dark lateral stripe. Photo by G. J. M. Timmerman.

of great importance to ichthyologists. *R. daniconius* and other related species from outlying areas of southeast Asia create a very large complex.

The fish is basically silver with overtones of creamy yellow to bronze-brown tinge towards the back while the fins are colorless. Just like most *Rasbora* it has a distinct lateral stripe. The stripe is variable in width and intensity of color. It may be reduced to a thin stripe, stay fairly wide,

A pair of *R. daniconius* in the throes of spawning amidst a clump of fine leafy plant which is indispensable in the breeding of these free spawners. Photo by R. Zukal.

or in some cases broken into sections resulting in a blotchy or spotted condition.

In captivity they are known to reach 8–9 cm in length although in the wild they can grow as long as 20 cm. Typical of the genus, the sexes are difficult to separate except during the adult stage when the female becomes distended with eggs and her body depth and thickness differ visibly from that of the males.

The lateral stripe of *R. daniconius* is quite variable appearing intensely in some or scarcely indicated in others. Photo by Dr. Herbert R. Axelrod.

The male eagerly positioning himself parallel to the female who is in the act of spawning over the bottom. Photo by R. Zukal.

Tail chasing is a conspicuous ritual prior to pairing. Photo by R. Zukal.

Those conditions which apply for the maintainance of most community fish suit this fish as well. The water temperature should range between 71° to 77°F., medium hard about 10 DH, neutral to slightly acid between pH 6 to 7. They are hardy fish and are able to temporarily withstand temperatures as low as 62°F. with little effect on their survival although their feeding and swimming activity will be diminished. They are resistant to many of the common fish diseases also.

In their native waters these fish are found in large schools near the surface and they spawn *en masse*. While in captivity if kept singly they become shy so it is advisable to keep several in a community tank with other peaceful fishes. Potential breeders should be pre-conditioned with such live food as *Daphnia*, *Cyclops*, insect larvae, etc. in addition to their regular diet of dried food. Prior to spawning the sexes should be kept separately or else they might spawn indiscriminately in the community tank.

Although the external appearance of the male and female is not different the sexes are separable by the relatively smaller and slenderer male in comparison to the larger and fuller female. Photo by Dr. H. R. Axelrod.

A male chasing the female from the rear at the start of courtship. Enough open space should be provided for this activity in setting up the spawning tank. Photo by R. Zukal.

Unlike other groups of fishes where the male embraces the female tightly such an action is only weakly accomplished in the courtship in *R. daniconius.* Photo by R. Zukal.

With the tail ready the male moves forward to get parallel to the female before the pair spawn simultaneously. Photo by R. Zukal.

The frenzy of spawning can be sufficiently strong to cause the pair to get entangled in the foliage. Make sure that plants are not placed too tightly so they can get out wihout injury. Photo by R. Zukal.

As soon as one spawning is over they are ready to move on to a new site usually selected by the female. Photo by R. Zukal.

After setting up a convenient sized spawning tank provided with fine leafy plants, clean water and a gravel substrate, one can proceed with the business of spawning them. It is best to keep the male overnight in the spawning tank and introduce the female the following morning; this way you will have the pleasure of observing the courtship ritual.

The male chases the female from the rear and she instinctively hides among the bushes. After a series of chases and male displays the two partners assume a side by side or parallel position to each other and the male makes an attempt to coil around the body of the female. This motion is not a complete coil for only his tail is visibly curved around the rear part of the female's body. The female seems to determine the spawning site where the eggs are shed amongst the leaves of the plants. The process is repeated with the female gliding through the greenery in

The pair leaving the planted area for some other suitable spawning place in the tank. (Below) The male stays close to the female until all the eggs are released. This takes several hours. Photos by R. Zukal.

As soon as these fishes lose interest with each other they will start eating the eggs and they should then be removed. This is easily determined for one will not see them in a side-by-side attitude as above any longer. Photo by R. Zukal.

search of other spawning sites. When spawning stops (after noontime in this case) the spawners should be removed for they may devour the spawn.

After a few days the eggs will start hatching into moderately sized fry. Not all the eggs are expected to hatch but as many as 200 to 300 young may hatch and on the 7th day they are free swimming at a temperature of 79°F. Just like the parents the young will accept live as well as dried prepared food provided they are small enough for them to swallow. Infusoria followed by newly hatched brine shrimp is a good first diet. Keep the tank protected from strong light. With optimum feeding conditions growth is rapid. Large amounts of food should be offered to avoid cannibalism. Sort them out according to size as soon as you think that the tank is too small for them. In about eight months they are ready to breed and are capable of spawning every three months.

Like most anabantids the tank requirements for keeping chocolate gouramis are not critical except for maintaining a fairly constant tropical temperaure. Photo by Dr. H. R. Axelrod.

The Chocolate Gourami

Sphaerichthys osphromenoides Canestrini

The chocolate gourami belongs to a group of unusually interesting and colorful fishes, the anabantids, a subdivision of the perch-like fishes. All anabantoids possess labyrinths which is a special organ of respiration found among these fishes. While the majority of fishes breathe solely by means of their gills which absorb oxygen dissolved in the water, a labyrinthine fish like the chocolate gourami in addition to the normal gill respiration is able to breathe atmospheric air. The labyrinth is an accessory respiratory organ found in the upper part of the gill region. It is composed of a complicated system of layers or lamella which are covered by a thin covering tissue richly supplied with blood capillaries. This is where the exchange of gases between the blood and the air takes place. Consequently, labyrinthine fishes can survive in places where the water is very poor in oxygen content, areas where oxygen has been depleted by decay, pollution, etc. With almost all labyrinths (anabantids), the use of atmospheric air is a necessity; if the fishes are trapped underwater they will drown.

Many of the anabantids like the bettas, gouramis, paradise fishes, etc. are much more colorful than our small, delicate and rather unimpressive and drab-looking *Sphaerichthys osphromenoides* but unlike these better known and well-studied fishes, our knowledge of the process of spawning and breeding behaviour of the chocolate gourami is still incomplete and, therefore, the fish still intrigues me.

This species was first described in 1860 but it is not too plentiful even in its habitat and is seldom found in even the bigger pet shops. The opportunity to observe their spawning behavior is limited. It has yet to be confirmed whether the chocolate gouramis all spawn the same way, or whether there are several different spawning techniques . . . or even whether observers are watching different fishes!!

Chocolate gouramis range in color from gray brown to deep chocolate brown according to their physical, psychological, and physiological state. Healthy individuals acquire a reddish cast. During spawning color changes occur. The dark parts of the body turn almost black while other areas become very pale as well. Several pale yellow irregular bands encircle the body the extent and number of which are very variable, and some irregular dark streaks are present on the fins. The ventral fins are produced into long slender filaments or "feelers". They also have "fright" color patterns.

In Sumatra and Malaya they are found in shallow, sluggish to stagnant ditches in the jungles or in the farms. These ditches are generally choked with dense vegetation

A chocolate gourami in good health acquires a reddish to pinkish color over the basic light brown color. Photo by R. Zukal.

Spawning fishes turn deep brown to black as the body stripes become much paler as represented in this photo by H. J. Richter.

A typical habitat of the chocolate gourami among the palm trees in Malaysia. High humidity and temperature characterize this environment. Photo by Dr. Herbert R. Axelrod.

and the bottom may be at times sandy but usually covered with mud and muck from rotting plant material. The water is usually mud-brown in color, soft, rich in humic acid but very poor in oxygen. The surrounding air is very heavy with moisture due to the prevailing high temperature in the area. So, if one expects to keep this gourami in perfect condition, these physical parameters should be kept in mind. They are peaceful fishes and may be kept with other species but being shy in disposition they are best kept by themselves. They have been taken from areas with a water hardness between 0.3 to 5 DH, a pH ranging from 5.5 to 7, and a temperature between 85° to 92°F. They succumb to temperatures lower than 76°F. but can tolerate comfortably high temperatures like 95°F. and they are susceptible to skin infections in captivity. Aeration is not necessary but an aquarium cover is needed to keep the hot humid air above the tank from escaping and to some extent block off too much light. A dark bottom is desirable and lots of plants preferably the weedy type should be included.

The natural food of chocolate gouramis are mosquito larvae and they will of course prefer such live foods as *Daphnia*, *Cyclops*, brine shrimp, worms, etc. over dried foods although they learn to accept the more convenient dried foods. However, only live food can pre-condition the fish for successful spawning.

Distinguishing the sexes is still a problem. One supposed index is the shape of the fins which unfortunately are seldom extended fully long enough for positive identification. Photo by G. Senfft.

Chocolate gouramis react quickly to most external stimuli eliciting the appearance of a "fright pattern" shown here. Photo by H. J. Richter.

These gouramis are naturally shy and they prefer to stay close to the surface among reed-like plants characteristic of their natural habitat. Photos by Dr. S. Frank.

Sex differences are difficult to recognize. It is reported that the intensity of the reddish parts of the male is greater and that his anal fin is deeper and his dorsal fin ends into a point whereas the same fin is blunt in the female. The size of the abdomen is not too useful for sex descrimination. A well fed male can be as broad as a female laden with eggs.

The spawning ritual is not typical for an anabantoid. The male lures the female by fin spreading and chasing in a circle. However unlike most anabantoids which build bubble nests, chocolate gouramis do not. They lay their eggs on the bottom rather than at the surface and they are mouth breeders. Oral incubation is known in some species of the genus *Betta*.

The released fry are large and can easily manage the nauplii of *Artemia*, the brine shrimp, or any other equivalent live food. With such a diet they grow very quickly and in less than two months may measure more than an inch long. Adults are rarely more than two inches long.

The only documented egg-laying of chocolate gouramis took place in an incident in which the author (HRA) was involved. This important event was recorded by several magazine articles which are reproduced here in case they contain some vital point which will assist you in spawning and rearing the fry of the chocolate gourami.

When sufficiently disturbed the white streaks on the body almost completely disappear. Photo by Dr. H. R. Axelrod.

Unlike most anabantoids the courtship in chocolate gouramis ultimately climaxes near the bottom and not close to the surface. Photo by R. Zukal.

In spite of the difficulty in identifying the sex it is relatively safe to presume the male chases the female as in most fishes. Photo by Dr. H. R. Axelrod.

Chocolate gouramis are peaceful and can be maintained as a group in one tank. Photo by Dr. S. Frank.

These fish in their natural environment consume large numbers of insect larvae but in captivity they will take most prepared dry or frozen foods. However, to keep them in spawning condition (like the lower fish) they require live food. Photos by Dr. S. Frank.

Spawning Chocolate Gouramis

Note: Dr. Herbert R. Axelrod and Mr. Hans J. Richter have documented, in a series of photographs, the actual spawning of the chocolate gourami but, unfortunately, not the emergence of the fry.

There is still a mystery about these fish since no documented rearing of young has ever taken place. It seems fairly certain that someday, someone will have success. Hopefully a later volume in this continuing series will be able to record the complete story. What is known to date (1973) follows with verbatim reprints of important TFH *Magazine articles.*

BY DR. HERBERT R. AXELROD
Photos by HANS JOACHIM RICHTER

In October, 1971, I was in Frankfurt, Germany, attending the world's largest book fair. So huge was this fair that 1,500 different publishers attended, with large display areas where each showed his wares to more than 100,000 buyers. Buses were needed to take people from one building to another on the special "Messegelände" or fair grounds where Frankfurt has its conventions.

While in Frankfurt I took this opportunity to visit my friend Heiko Bleher. Heiko worked in Florida for a few years raising rare water plants for me, having spent most of his youth in Brazil with his famous mother (Lotus Osiris) collecting and cultivating Brazilian water plants. Heiko has his own business now, Aquarium Rio, on Frankfurter Strasse 33, 6231 Niederhochstadt, Germany. He specializes in rare, well-acclimated fishes . . . and he certainly does have them!

The "fright pattern" is also characterized by the darkening of the head and eye region. Photo by G. Wolfsheimer.

Heiko invited Evelyn and me to visit a typical Brazilian houseparty churrasco (barbecue) and it was great fun cooking spareribs while the temperature was almost 0° outside. Of course I stayed inside and acted as the lazy guest and official taster!

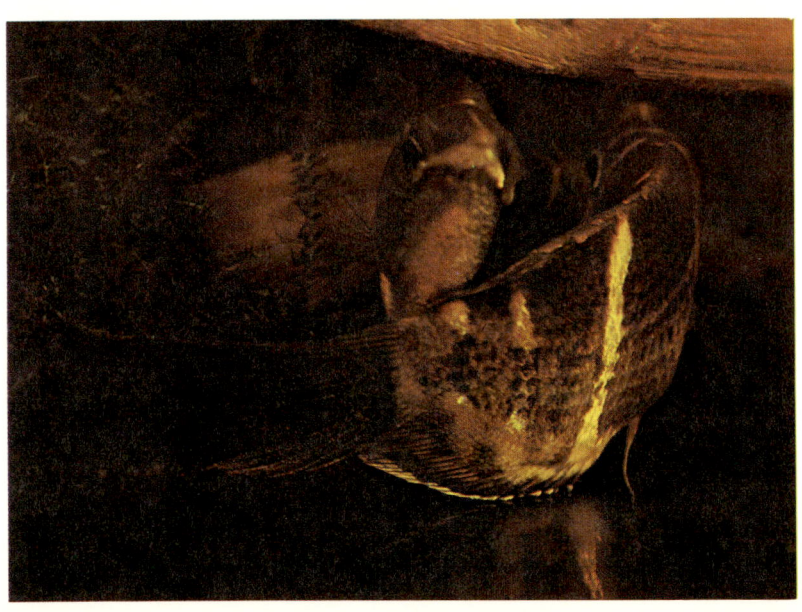

At the culmination of the embrace the two fish are coiled about each other like cupped hands, bodies almost touching the bottom ready to spawn any moment. Photo by H. J. Richter.

(Facing page) The spawning embrace is typically anabantoid in all respects save that it occurs quite close to the bottom instead of near the surface. Photos by H. J. Richter.

While discussing fishes with Heiko, the conversation got around to my planned visit the next day to Leipzig, East Germany, where I wanted to visit my friend Hans Joachim Richter. Until that evening, I thought it would be impossible to visit East Germany without a special visa, as conversations with the American embassy in Frankfurt and Berlin resulted in conclusions that it would be better if I stayed out of East Germany since it took a long time to get a visa, etc. I mentioned this to Heiko and he laughed.

"Just drive to the border and you'll get a visa in an hour," he said

Well, the border was only a few hours away by car, so off we went, fully prepared to just drive to the border, get a polite "Sorry . . . no visa . . . no visit," and return to Frankfurt. After all, it was such a nice crisp period of the year, with the trees turning golden red, so we considered it an outing.

Before we left for the border . . . just in case we got through . . . I brought along some of Heiko's fishes which I thought would surely challenge Hans Joachim Richter's skills in breeding fishes and photographing them while they were doing their thing. Heiko gave me a dozen chocolate gouramis, *Sphaerichthys osphromenoides*. No one had ever verified how they spawn.

When we got to the border, showed our passports without visas, and explained that we just wanted to visit Richter in Leipzig, the friendly border guards cooperated and issued us a visa. Getting the visa was only a question of paying the fee, paying in advance for a hotel room and food for the days we wanted to stay in East Germany, buying insurance for our car in case we had an accident, and clearing customs. The visa took an hour . . . clearing customs took several hours. It seems there was nothing in their guide books about bringing in live tropical fishes . . . calls were made to Berlin and other eastern German towns housing the authorities, until in desperation, we were allowed to bring in the fish.

The famous Hitler-built Autobahns in Germany were the world's first super-highways. Hitler built them in Germany to connect every major German city, as part of his war-preparations. The Autobahns have no speed limits and I went sailing down the highway at 120 miles per hour in my rented Mercedes-Benz. I made the border in two hours from Frankfurt, and when I got to the East German side of the Autobahn, I just kept speeding along at the same 120 miles per hour (200 km/hr). Little did I know that the speed limit throughout East Germany is half that speed and that speeders are promptly arrested and severely fined! That must have been my lucky day, for I passed hundreds of small, under-powered East German Warburg cars, but never was I stopped by the polizei!

Finally, that afternoon, I met Hans Joachim Richter and his charming wife and two children. Hans is an engineer whose specialty is the heating of outdoor pipes to keep them from freezing. His wife teaches Russian, and his children are still in elementary school. Hans lives in a most comfortable four room apartment, with one room used as a fish room. He was positively delighted when he saw the chocolate gouramis and the various African cichlids I had brought with me.

"These chocolate gouramis are ready to spawn," Hans announced.

"I don't think so," I said.

"They are very easy to spawn. Especially when they are in such good condition as these. I'll spawn them and send you the pictures. OK?"

Of course I said "Yes", but I didn't think it would be that easy.

I left East Germany two days later and the day after I left Hans Joachim Richter spawned the chocolate gouramis and sent me the photographs to prove it. Hans is still writing the complete story about the spawning and rearing of the chocolate gourami, and after he has repeated the spawning a few times more and gotten some better photos,

An embracing pair underneath a log on the bare bottom of the tank. Photo by H. J. Richter.

Sphaerichthys osphromenoides eggs photographed for the first time, are unusually large and are deposited on the bottom as the fish circle each other. Photo by H. J. Richter.

he'll do a special feature for TFH, but in the meantime Hans Joachim Richter has proven that the chocolate gourami pair spawn in a relatively naked tank, without plants or sand but with a log under which they spawn, with a high temperature of about 85°F. The pair embrace on the bottom where it is dark and sheltered. A dozen or two large, amber eggs are released during the embrace, and one of the pair picks up the eggs in its mouth and broods them. The mouth-pouch extends the profile of the fish, and the fish constantly snatches air from the surface and forces the air over the eggs, passing the air out through its operculum.

There are so many more details we want to know . . . where does fertilization take place . . . does the male or female or both carry the eggs . . . how long does it take to hatch . . . how do you raise the young . . . what are the sex differences of the fish . . . how often do they spawn . . .???

We'll just have to wait for Hans to finish writing his story. He said it might take six months more, as when Hans Joachim Richter does something *he does it right!*

Hans and I have something special between us and this fish. About ten years ago when I gave a speech in Czechoslovakia, Hans told me that he often spawned the chocolate gourami. Trying to be as polite as I could, I told Hans that I didn't believe him . . . it must have been another fish, and that he should learn to take fish spawning photographs to prove his stories and share his knowledge with others. I had never expected that Hans was able to take fish pictures or that he could spawn the chocolate gourami. I was wrong on both accounts. Sharing the honors with Ruda Zukal, these two gentlemen are undoubtedly the most prolific and most talented aquarium photographers the world has ever known.

I can hardly wait to present to you the details which Hans has promised me . . . perhaps with better photographs, too!

The Chocolate Gourami
Sphaerichthys osphromenoides Canestrini 1860

Observations on the Mating Behavior

BY HANS JOACHIM RICHTER, Leipzig, DDR

The breeding of gouramis is continually presented by experienced breeders as free of problems. To this should be added that basically every fish or quite generally every animal can be bred. This requires only that the optimal conditions be provided for the animal involved. That has been shown often enough. For many animals, including the fishes, the *required conditions* with minor corrections are adequate. On the other hand, there are also many animals for which *living conditions* must be provided, but only at great cost, apart from the fact that one does not know the *natural conditions* one hundred percent. The "recipes" which are often given in the literature do not provide sufficient information. Therefore, one must attempt to learn as much as possible from all sources about the native habitats. The best breeders are therefore, even today, to be found among those who intensively study the technical literature, as well as that of peripheral sciences.

Let us return to the labyrinthines. Besides the multiplicity of labyrinthine fishes which can really be relatively easily kept and bred under the given conditions, there are nevertheless also some kinds which have not been bred yet. To these belong the mysterious chocolate gourami. This has been reported on for decades and often in such a way as to seduce the ordinary aquarist to buy the quite expensive fishes, since the difficulties of keeping them are discussed again and again, quite apart from the contradictory reports on breeding or mating behavior. So let's thumb through the literature:

Within a short time all the eggs are carefully mouthed. This photo is concrete evidence of the mouthbrooding behaviour of this anabantoid. Photo by H. J. Richter.

With the eggs safely hidden in the mouth the fish moves towards the surface to swallow some air which evidently not only provides air for respiration of the fish but also to aerate the eggs. Photo by H. J. Richter.

In 1906 the Wochenschrift published an article: "*Luciocephalus pulcher*, livebearing pike from Sumatra and *Osphronemus malayanus*, livebearing Gourami from the Malayan Peninsula and from Sumatra" by Julius Reichelt, Berlin.

J. Reichelt reported in this article that he traveled to Sumatra three times especially for chocolate Gourami, among other things, and everytime brought fine, large specimens to Singapore, but, on the trip back to Berlin, the fishes always perished because of sudden cold and other situations. He did bring back to Berlin several fishes from his last trip, but these, likewise, died within a week.

He wrote, further, that he had caught chocolate Gourami in ditches and puddles about six to ten miles from the coast. The water in these water spots was supposed to have been as dark as black coffee. Because of partial changes of water in Singapore, involving addition of clear water, he was supposed to have had repeated losses. In Singapore he was also supposed to have captured two small marine fishes, thereby leading him to mix in (1/10) sea water. This was probably successful, since he brought about 20 fishes in good shape back to Hamburg. On the long sea voyage all of the dying females delivered 25 to 40 young which were supposed to have been as colorful as the older fishes. The young were also supposed to have eaten "the tiniest live food" after several hours. The young fish were supposed to have been well guarded by the parents for the first week. Since Reichelt never saw how the young suddenly arrived, he believed he was dealing with livebearers.

In the same year Reichelt once again wrote about the chocolate Gourami in reply to several critics in the Wochenschrift, whereby he indicates he could be dealing with mouth-breeders, but which he nevertheless considered to be unlikely.

Johann Paul Arnold (Hamburg) wrote as early as 1939 on the chocolate Gourami, now by the proper scientific name, *Sphaerichthys osphromenoides*. He wrote that in 1934 the importer Otto Winkelmann (Hamburg-Altona) introduced seven specimens which were passed on to the novelty breeder Hoffmann. These fishes, too, failed to breed. The chocolate Gourami imported regularly later by the Hamburg Aquarium also failed to reproduce. Arnold offered his book "Foreign Freshwater Fish" as a prize for the first breeder of the "Malayan Gourami."

Arnold published another article in the DATZ in 1949. In this article Arnold reported on a breeding report by Aaran Wold from America. Among other things, this breeding report states:

"Color display reached its climax on December 26, about five weeks after the purchase of the fish. At this time the male begins to build a bubble nest, whereupon the depth of the water was reduced by half. A considerable amount of muck had accumulated, but only a small portion of it was involved. Spawning began on the morning of December 27, 1948. The male violently drove the female under the nest, and then embraced her with his body in typical Gourami fashion. The eggs, about a hundred, were carefully brought together under the nest and cared for by the male. After spawning the female was removed. At a temperature of 80°F. (27°C.) the young hatched in three days. Ten days after spawning, the male was removed from the tank. A large mass of *Nitella* was added to the tank just after the young had hatched. The yolk of a hard-boiled egg, pressed through a muslin cloth, was the principal food for the young. The layer of mud on the bottom and the micro-organisms which developed from the *Nitella* supplemented the diet. In three weeks the young fish took newly hatched microcultures. Their diet was supplemented by liver protein preparation. Unfortunately, a short-circuit in the heater destroyed almost all of the young—except ten—when they were three months old. By the end of the sixth month I still had four young fishes which had attained about two-thirds the size of their parents."

As Arnold wrote, he had no reason to doubt the correctness of these details, particularly since his informant was supposed to be a member of the San Francisco Scientific Society.

Likewise, an article by Racowics appeared in 1949 in America in which he reported how, in a shipment of 300 chocolate Gourami which he kept in an aquarium, he discovered many young on the following morning. He put two, fine, fully grown specimens (which were at first meant for dissection) into alcohol, alive, whereby they spat out fry which were 4 mm in size.

After these early observations, another rather unauthenicated article on chocolate Gourami appeared in the DATZ in 1955, by Bahr. He wrote that

1. A nest is prepared under a floating plant, and done so in such a way that the accumulated air bubbles coalesce into one air bubble;
2. The fishes embrace under this air bubble, whereby the male presses the side of the female;

3. The eggs float to the surface directly into the nest;
4. The male cares for the brood from three to six days, and continually improves the nest (what, the bubble?—the author).

This all could very well be dreamed up because, first of all, it is hardly to be assumed that the "observed" fishes could have been another kind of fish, for the author would have noted that the fish pictured in the article mentioned are not identical with the observed ones. The fishes illustrated were chocolate Gourami in all cases. Secondly, one and the same fish does not have different eggs . . . certainly not with such gross differences but with no differences in maturation time (aside from the slight differences because of water temperature).

The first correct observations are found in the book "Exotics in the Aquarium" by A. von den Nieuwenhuizen, and in great detail re: the errors in confusing the sexes in an article by Dr. E. Schmidt, published in the journal "Tropische Fische" in 1962.

Two years ago I again had chocolate Gourami which spawned. At that time I first determined unequivocally that I had never before possessed a male. Previously, therefore, females had spawned together, thus resulting in some data in my article in the AT at that time. The poor photograph with my article in the AT clearly showed a female with the eggs in the throat pouch, and not—as I then wrote—a male. So much for the literature.

Almost two years I waited in vain for news from my friends in the German Federal Republic and abroad that someone had chocolate Gouramis for me. Since my friend Dr. Herbert R. Axelrod informed me that he wanted to visit me, I asked him, among other things, to bring me chocolate Gouramis. On the afternoon of October 19, 1971 Dr. Axelrod met with me, and the first thing that he pulled out of the shipping carton he had brought was a bag of chocolate Gourami—twelve of them. Dr. Axelrod gave them to me with the comment: "I would now like to learn the truth about chocolate Gouramis from you." I was able to report that, because of the attentiveness of my wife, I was able to observe these fish spawning.

The twelve specimens were placed in a tank without a bottom layer. The water was completely desalted and supplemented with Torumin, and then was run a while over a peat filter. Thus the water was quite coffee-brown, and rich in humic acid. Water temperature was adjusted to about 28°C. with an immersible boiler, and held at this temperature with a heater.

Based upon a study of the literature, I was convinced that chocolate Gouramis had to be found in similar water conditions in their native habitat. The first two days the fishes were shy, hiding themselves as soon as someone entered the room. It seemed, however, that the chocolate Gourami felt rather comfortable in this tank, for they showed their best coloration immediately. I was also able to observe mating behavior of several fishes on the following days. That inspired me especially since I noted that the superfluous males continually disturbed the mating pair—to set up an extra pair, and, above all, to attempt to photograph the spawning behavior.

Therefore I set up a tank on October 24, 1971. Since I knew that chocolate Gourami spawn on the bottom, I installed a black PVC plate in the tank in order to better observe the spawning. Towards 11:00 I placed a randomly selected pair in this tank which was filled with the same water that was in the tank mentioned further above, and which contained other fish.

This separately placed pair immediately began mating behavior. I therefore adequately fed the fishes with *Cyclops* and *Enchytraeus*.

Since the pair began mating behavior in a short time, I photographed it, and at about 8 p.m. was able to photograph actual spawning.

Here is the precise course of spawning:
Chocolate Gourami mating behavior usually occurs when the fishes meet in the tank. All fins are spread and the fishes circle. After a circuit both fishes then swim together to the spawning-ground-to-be on the bottom. Here, the chocolate Gourami circle around several times with spread fins, then swim apart again, each in another direction.

About 7:45 p.m. after swimming in ever-decreasing circles, whereby the PVC plate at this spot was quite cleanly polished by the trailing anals, simulated mating occurred. During the simulated mating the male swam into a loop made by the curved and somewhat inclined body of the female. But this also happened the other way around, too. The caudal fin of the male becomes almost black and the female continues to inflate the reddish throat pouch. Both fishes, in their excitement, hold their mouths open. It is then that one first notes that the mouth is not as small as it seems at first appearance. The simulated mating behavior is interrupted only when the partners go for air.

At 8 p.m. I noticed that, as the male swam into the loop made by the female, he trembled slightly. Since I was familiar with this action, I knew that the male was releasing sperm. The female now had to lay the eggs immediately. And this actually occurred. I estimated about 80 eggs. For about 30 seconds both fishes remained motionless near the eggs, then separated somewhat from one another. Now the female began to collect the eggs slowly. The eggs are relatively large and cream-colored. After the first 20 to 30 eggs were collected, the remainder was gathered ever more slowly; but not all the eggs could be fitted in the greatly distended throat pouch. The female swam to the surface of the water for air, and stayed there. The male approached the eggs and took one. I thought at first that he was going to eat up the left-over eggs. But this was not the case. The male swam to the female and spit out the egg directly in front of her snout. And the female really snapped up the egg and put it into her throat pouch. By continually "chewing", she made room for all the other eggs which the male brought to her. At this point the female's throat pouch was quite distended, and she frequently, and deeply, took in air. Meanwhile she swam restlessly up and down the glass side. So much for the mating behavior of the chocolate Gourami.

You can well imagine that I waited anxiously for the result of the spawning. The following morning the throat pouch of the female was just as swollen as it was after she had collected the eggs. That evening the other pair spawned. It was only by the third morning that the distension of the throat pouch subsided. I put food in the tank and the female ate immediately. Within six days five pairs spawned, but always with the same result: on the third day the female's throat pouch was empty again. This is still puzzling. Further experimentation will hopefully shed some light on this.

It is to be said, concerning the keeping of chocolate Gourami, that these fish can be kept well in the most varied kinds of water over long periods. The longest aquarium life, however, of these fish was when they were in water supplemented with humic acid. Native waters are supposed to have a hardness of 0.5 to 3° DH and a pH between 5 and 6. Flying prey probably makes up almost all of the chocolate Gourami's nutrition, so it seems appropriate to feed the fishes *Drosophila* or fly larvae. Almost all food which can be taken, even dry food, is eaten.

Now for the sexual differences in chocolate Gourami. Here, too, much has been written, and none was quite clear as to which sex was involved. One must take into consideration, however, that—based upon the small lots of purchased specimens—often only one of the sexes have been seen, not the other. This was my case for several years. Sexual characteristics were sought and even found in the small lots when the females spawned together. Thus, various figures depict the females as males, or vice versa.

The color pictures of this species finally show clearly that confusion of the sexes is hardly possible. As in the case of many labyrinthine fishes, the dorsal, above all, can be used for differentiating the sexes. The dorsal end comes to a point in the male, but is rounded in the female. This will not always enable differentiation; for this the fishes must spread their fins. The fins are usually equally long when folded. For this reason, a further distinction in fins can be used: in the males the fins are edged in white, while this is not the case in females.

Differentiation based upon the narrow or broad part of the abdomen in well-fed fishes is hardly possible, and even possible light, longitudinal streaks do not represent sexual characteristics.

The following observations are interesting:

If one keeps several chocolate Gouramis in a tank, and there are some males among them, one can always see the males are quite quarrelsome. In their quarrels some rather serious biting occurs, and it is not advisable to keep several males together in one tank.

If chocolate Gouramis are kept in small tanks where they cannot flee into protective corners at the slightest supposed danger, then their colors pale with lightning speed when they are frightened. The fishes show a yellow-brown basic color with a few dark spots on the body. Chocolate Gouramis exhibit similar coloration when they sleep. In both cases, a protective coloration is involved whereby the fishes adapt to their environment.

It is not difficult to realize why this fish deserves the name red top cichlid. Photo by Dr. H. R. Axelrod.

The Red Top Cichlid

Labeotropheus trewavasae Fryer

In appearance *Labeotropheus trewavasae* and *L. fuelleborni* are so close that they are considered as two very nearly related species or "sibling species." Both are found in Lake Malawi, home of the now famous mbuna (em-boo-na) or shore fishes of this African rift lake. Intensive field work and detailed study of many preserved specimens was required before the identity of *L. trewavasae* was confirmed and that it is not synonymous to the more common algal feeder *L. fuelleborni*.

So similar are the structures of the mouth parts that if the rest of their bodies were cut off it will be quite difficult to tell these two species part. They occupy the same ecological

When startled the bars of the red top can turn pale as other areas like the head becomes markedly darker. Photo by H. Hansen. (Below) Normal coloration. Photo by Dr. D. Terver.

After the territory of each fish is established different species of mbunas tolerate each other within the limits of the territory. Upper fish, *Pseudotropheus auratus*; lower fish, *L. trewavasae*. Photo by Dr. D. Terver.

zone of the lake, mainly the rocky zone, and to some degree the vegetative zone. They eat the same type of food. With their highly specialized mouth parts they scrape algae off the rocks and leaves of the plants and yet they also feed on small invertebrates.

Labeotropheus trewavasae differs from *L. fuelleborni* principally on body proportions, meristics or numerical counts and variations of some parts of the body like the spines and scales and on coloration. The Red Top is more slender almost cylindrical in body shape in comparison to the

L. trewavasae, one of the most attractive Malawian cichlids was unknown until 1956. The female may be speckled, lower photo or resemble the male. Photos by Dr. D. Terver.

The "barred" form of male, upper fish and the "peppered" form of female, lower fish. Photo by Dr. H. R. Axelrod.

The original barred condition of this "speckled" form is obscured by the development of spots in some females only. Photo by H. Hansen.

shorter more stocky *fuelleborni*. Consequently the scale and dorsal fin counts are higher in *trewavasae*. The males of *trewavasae* are indigo blue with 6 transverse bands or more (12 bands have been seen in some individuals) with the red dorsal fin from whence the common name originated.

Polymorphism similar to that of *fuelleborni* also exists in this species. Two types of females, in a ratio of 1 : 1 in the natural population, has been reported. One female form is barred like the male but the body color and bars are paler; the other form is bicolored with black and orange spots or flecks on a light gray or dirty white background and which are described as the speckled or peppered types. The usual cichlid markings on the fins (egg dummies) are present in both sexes. The mechanism and extent of polymorphism in *Labeotropheus* are still not fully known.

Just like any other mbuna the Red Tops need large aquaria and well oxygenated, preferably alkaline, and clean water. This Malawian will, of course, also be content in soft water, the same kind as in its home; among the rift lakes of Africa Lake Malawi has the least amount of dissolved minerals. However, some aquarists suggest neutral to hard water for these fish as a means of controlling a fungus disease to which they are quite susceptible. Hard water has not been found detrimental to their spawning capabilities. A pile of large rocks with many crevices for hiding, some smooth rocks on a bottom of coarse gravel, plenty of light and a few plants like *Vallisneria* all taken together will certainly create an atmosphere similar to that of their natural habitat. Extreme fluctuations in pH and temperature should be avoided. A temperature drop to 71°F. is enough to kill the young and inhibit the development of the eggs.

Another variant of the "speckled" form of *L. trewavasae* with much lighter body background. Photo by Dr. D. Terver.

A male red top in spawning condition (lower fish), will defend his territory from all intruders. Note the very distinct "egg spot" on the anal fin. Photo by W. Hoppe.

Fungus infections if caught early enough are controllable by antifungal drugs and additional aeration.

It is not difficult to tell whether the fish is ready to spawn or not. The male red top cichlid starts showing brighter coloration and spends most of his time cleaning the surface of rocks and digging shallow pits around his territory. He is much more prone to chase intruders and pursues females so persistently that unwilling females may at times be injured. Ripe females, in addition to having slightly bulging abdomens, have a prominent genital papilla a few days before spawning.

An aquarium similar to the community tank in all aspects except for smaller size (20 gallons or less) can be set up for spawning and as a place where the female can brood the eggs and where the young can grow away from the large predatory adults.

At the height of the spawning stage, the dorsal fin of the male becomes more vivid red and his body turns iridescent indigo blue. Photo by Dr. H. R. Axelrod.

Spotting occurs among females only and is never present prior to sexual differentiation. Photo by Dr. H. R. Axelrod.

A barred female of *L. trewavasae* brooding as indicated by the swollen throat area. Photo by Dr. D. Terver.

If the selected fish are ready they can engage in the mating ritual once they are placed together. The male displays by making a violent turn or twist within sight of the female and she responds by moving closer almost touching him and they encircle each other several times in either left or right direction. During these motions they are also slowly moving towards the bottom, closer to the spawning site. Previously cleaned areas are preferred but this may be dispensed with since there is not enough time for the male to establish a territory in the spawning tank. Do not forget to place a few smooth-surfaced rocks upon which the eggs can be safely laid. When the eggs are laid on the gravel or sandy bottom the female picks up not only the eggs but also some grains of sand, bits of gravel or other detrital matter which may damage the eggs.

The spawning position is easily recognized. Either the male or the female assumes a position describing a **T** in relation to the other. The head is held very close or even touching the genital region of the other. Trial runs can occur with no eggs laid. During actual spawnings the T position lasts a few seconds longer accompanied by slight quiverings or tremors of the body as the female lays a few eggs and the male ejects some milt. The female immediately picks up the eggs carefully and stores them in her mouth cavity. Spawnings continue further but positions alternate thus the eggs in the mouth of the female may come in contact with more milt whenever she has her head near the male genital opening. Presumably she is attracted by the brightly colored "egg spots" on the anal fin of the male.

The territorial habits, aggressiveness and reproductive behavior of the red top cichlid are typical for a mbuna cichlid but they lay fewer eggs, as few as 10 eggs or 40 at most, in comparison to *fuelleborni*. The female also could

L. trewavasae eggs incubated 24 hours after spawning. Photo by Dr. D. Terver.

A female speckled form of *L. trewavasae* brooding. Photo by H. Hansen.

habitually jettison a whole batch of eggs and deliberately refuse to take them back into her mouth. On the other hand, designed threats might not cause her to drop her brood. The incubation period lasts about 23 days, at times longer. The length of incubation is influenced by such factors as temperature, size and age of the female.

The developing fry and the female can be kept together as long as a month. A few days following the first emergence of the fry from the buccal pouch the female usually accepts the young fish at night and keeps them until the following morning. She rarely shows aggression to her young unless she is starved. The fry will eat the same type of food as the adults but of smaller size, of course.

The terminal mouth initially present in the fry is shifted to the ventral position characteristic of the genus *Labeotropheus* at 3 months of age. The sex differences are noticeable in about a year at which time they are ready to spawn.

A telescope-eyed veiltail goldfish is just one of the hundreds of varieties produced by the domestication of the wild type of goldfish. Photo by H. Hansen.

Goldfish

Carassius auratus

One of the oldest of domesticated fishes is the goldfish. Its history as a pet goes back for many centuries, and it is not quite certain where the fish came from originally since nothing exists in nature which is identical to any of the goldfish we see in every petshop in the world.

Tubercles appear in the gill region of the male goldfish, left fish during the breeding season. Photo by R. Zukal.

The pre-spawning chase shown below and on the facing page starts slowly but will increase in tempo and may take the pair to any part of the tank. Photos by R. Zukal.

Garden pools for goldfish should be adequately deep to provide refuge when the temperature of the water gets too high or too low.

Breeding and maintaining goldfish is easy and I can remember during my school days how I had so much fun with a pair of goldfish kept in a small glass jar. In the springtime, when the male developed tubercles (white "pimples") on his gill cover, all I had to do to stimulate the goldfish to spawn was add a little hot water to its bowl. In about 30 minutes the fish would spawn, splashing so much water it disrupted the class (which was my goal at that time).

Sexing fancy goldfish is very difficult for the beginner, especially when he is faced with the round body types such are illustrated in this chapter.

While it is possible to breed your goldfish all year round, I don't suggest that you do this since the spawns are small and it is just too much trouble. It is better to separate the sexes from September until April or May (of course if you live in South Africa, Australia or New Zealand your seasons are opposite to mine), and just put the fish together a few times during the spring and summer. While the fish are being separated they must be fed high protein foods and, while live foods are not necessary, they are very welcome in the goldfish's diet. In the spring the male will develop the nuptial tubercles on his gill cover and this indicates his readiness to spawn.

Fancy fish like the telescope-eyed goldfish peeking out of the water here need room to develop fully.

The pair moving towards a weedy part of the tank and, below, side-to-side and with violent fin flapping both fish spawn freely and simultaneously. Photos by R. Zukal.

The male stimulates the female by rubbing his rough gill plate against her head or abdomen during the process of spawning. Shown in both photos. Photos by R. Zukal.

Calico veiltail goldfish. Photo by Dr. H. R. Axelrod. Bubble-eyed goldfish. Photo by H. Hansen.

Telescope-eyed veiltail goldfish. Photo by H. Hansen.
Oranda goldfish. Photo by H. Hansen.

The turbulent spawning of goldfish depicted here often results in some torn fins, lost scales and a few broken plants. Photos by R. Zukal.

The force of spawning hurls the eggs about ultimately falling on the leaves or to the bottom and below, fins almost entangled, spawning continues unabated. Photos by R. Zukal.

surprising how easy the eggs come flying out into a soup plate. Once I have the eggs, I squirt the male's sperm onto them, swish the whole thing around (I had the soup plate half filled with clean, aged water) for a minute or two, then dump the whole spawn into a large aquarium and follow the steps I outlined above.

Goldfish are beautiful and peaceful and there is no reason why you cannot keep a pair or two in your tropical aquarium where they even serve as excellent scavengers.

Everything I have written here applies equally to all of the many colors, shapes and sizes of goldfish, both plain and fancy.

Male goldfish develop pearl-like tubercles on the gill plate. Some females may develop them but this is not a common occurrence. Photo by L. Perkins.

The proper way of holding a female goldfish intended to be spawned by hand. Photos by L. Perkins.

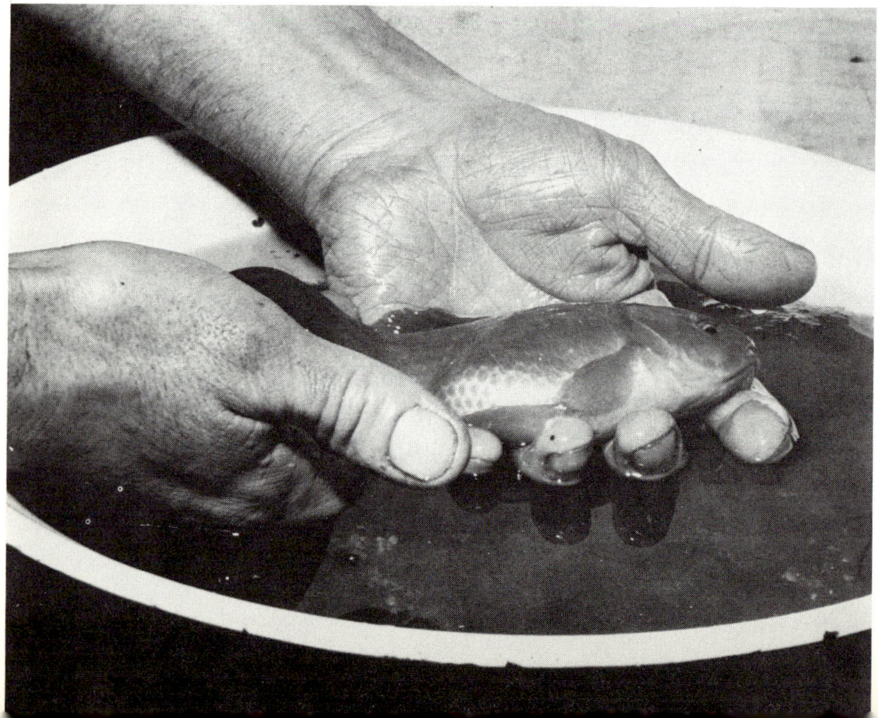

The ova are released with the aid of some slight pressure applied on the abdomen.

A similar pressure on a ripe male goldfish will release the milt, resembling a white milky substance, through the anal opening.

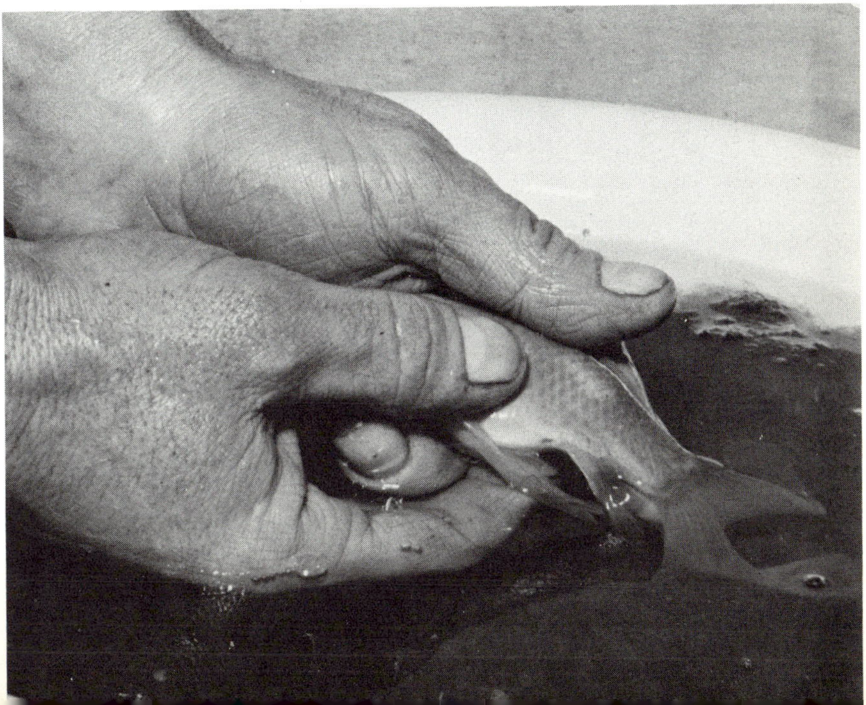

Normally the iris is yellow but it turns bright red in the adult chanchito shown here guarding the young. Photo by G. Marcuse.

The Chanchito

Cichlasoma facetum Jenyns

The chanchito or "little pig" as *C. facetum* is popularly known in its range is one of the many cichlids to be found in South America. It is native to southern Brazil (Rio Grande do Sul, Rio Parana), Paraguay, Uruguay, and northern Argentina. This species is also at times called "chameleon fish" because it can change its colors quickly, but many *Cichlasoma* have this same ability.

Just like many fishes, the best coloration is displayed by the males during the breeding season. The body has a background color of bronze to greenish yellow marked by a series of irregular black vertical bands and the edge of the dorsal and caudal fins are red. The body color can lighten or darken and can appear dull or iridescent. The iris of the eye is yellow in an immature fish, but turns red at the onset of sexual maturation. Sex differences are not recognizable

Chanchitos are known to uproot plants so other decorations are traditionally used such as bricks, stones, etc.
Photo by G. Marcuse.

The vertical fins of the male chanchito, above, are longer and more pointed than those of the female below. Photos by G. Marcuse.

The fry are guarded for a period of time by either chanchito parent. Presumably the bold coloration and pattern of substrate brooders keep the fry from straying.
Photo by G. Marcuse.

among the young individuals. In adult males the vertical fins are drawn out into points and the genital papilla is pointed whereas in a female chanchito the fins are rounded and the genital papilla is blunt.

Most cichlids are aggressive and this one is no exception. This fish is pugnacious, quarrelsome and can harass other fishes to death. They tear up poorly anchored plants in a tank so it is better to forego the desire to have plants in the set up. The tanks should be large (40–60 gallons) to give smaller and weaker fish some chance to avoid their pursuers. Water conditions are not very critical. They can tolerate reasonable fluctuations in pH and water hardness. The

The guarding instinct is particularly strong during the immediate period after hatching. This urge decreases with the passage of time and starved parents will invariably devour their young. Photo by G. Marcuse.

temperature of course should be tropical, between 75° and 85°F. To satisfy their digging instinct a course gravel bottom will be ideal. Flat slabs of stone, a flower pot or two, or a cured piece of hollow tree trunk can be included. They serve not only as decorations but possible spawning substrates as well. The niches created by these materials are also good hiding places.

Selecting the kind of food to give these greedy fish is never a problem. They eat many types of food including insects, worms, certain tadpoles and even dog and cat food.

However, the diet should be supplemented by vegetable matter such as spinach, lettuce, algae and oatmeal can be given too. The standard aquarium diet is recommended.

They are easy to breed (*C. facetum* was the first cichlid bred in captivity) and they could easily reproduce in the holding tanks without any supervision. But, if one decides to spawn them in a smaller container for closer observation, the intended parents must be carefully chosen. The size of the fish should be comparable and the reaction of one fish to the other must be observed. A weak or small female can be killed outright during the first encounter. A male and a female chanchito can be conditioned to each other's presence by placing them in a single tank but separated from each other by a transparent glass or plastic pane. Thus, they are physically separated but not visually and one can thereby

Cichlasoma nigrofasciatum is a species confused with the chanchito. Photo by W. Bechtle.

see their reactions to each other. The pane can be removed as one feels that the female is acceptable. At times several trials are needed before the male shows signs of true mating interests towards the female. It is also known that those fish which grew up together from the same shoal are generally more compatible.

Like a typical cichlid the male chanchito courts the female aggressively. A bright color display, fin spreading and fin wagging and ultimately pairing near the spawning site (which is usually the surface of the stone or any other place including the walls of the aquarium) is the usual result. The female lays a few adhesive eggs at a time. These are

The color pattern of a female guarding her fry.
Photo by G. Marcuse.

immediately fertilized. The release of the sexual products is accompanied by tremors along the body of the fish. Spawning is repeated until all the eggs are laid and as soon as this is accomplished, both fish brood over the eggs. They clean off any foreign material adhering to the eggs and carefully take them into their mouths and put them back again. They keep the water about the eggs in motion by constantly moving their pectoral fins like a fan thereby oxygenating the developing embryos. If there are other fishes about, the male chases them off to a safe distance.

Hatching occurs in eight to nine days later depending on the temperature. Of course not all the eggs are fertile but as many as sixty fry can result from one spawning. The parents do not keep the fry in the spawning site but will transfer them to a shallow depression on the substrate which they have previously diligently prepared. The fry remain in the hole for about a week guarded by their parents. During this period the yolk sac is gradually absorbed. Once the fry are able to swim freely they will be searching for an external source of nutrition. The fry should now be given small live food as brine shrimp nauplii or the nauplii of *Daphnia*, *Cyclops*, or small insect larvae. As they grow they can be changed to the diet of the adults. The fry will stay near the parents who keep them as a group like a sheep herder. The affinity between them weakens as time goes on. The young become more independent especially during feeding.

As soon as one notices that the parents ignore the fry it is wise to remove them for they could make a meal of their own young. The little chanchitos could now also be given more living space. Weather permitting they can be kept out-of-doors in large tubs or garden pools during the whole summer, providing the temperature remains over 70°F. In such containers they grow faster than when confined in small tanks indoors. In their habitat they grow to a length of twelve inches but in captivity they only reach a size of eight inches.

The female *Rivulus cylindraceus* is easily identified by the prominent ocellus on the top of the base of the tail. Photo by Dr. S. Frank.

All sick fish like this deformed Cuban rivulus should never be utilized for spawning. Photo by R. Zukal.

A pair of *R. cylindraceus* in all appearances ready for spawning. Photo by G. Senfft.

Cuban Rivulus

Rivulus cylindraceus Poey

The genus *Rivulus* belongs to the family of egg laying tooth carps Cyprinodontidae and it is a widely distributed genus in the southern United States, Central America and South America and includes numerous small but colorful species.

The color pattern of the male becomes more marked in the presence of a female elsewhere in the tank and below, whom he chases vigorously. Photos by R. Zukal.

Having overtaken the female the male pauses but below, the female decides to move away, for the moment at least. Photos by R. Zukal.

Still visibly laden with eggs the female is busily inspecting a possible site as the male darkens indicating his readiness to spawn. Photo by R. Zukal.

Although *Rivulus cylindraceus* is normally a native of Cuban freshwater streams, its range is within the limits of the United States (Florida) and it occasionally finds its way into aquarium fish dealers' tanks. It is a species not actively sought after by aquarists yet they are pretty, relatively non-aggressive, easy to keep and simple to breed. Due to its small size it does not require a large aquarium.

These fishes are mature with a body length of just over 2 inches (6 cm). The females are a trifle larger than the males as a rule. As in all the Cyprinodontidae the males are darker and more colorful than the females particularly during breeding. Both sexes have lateral stripes interspersed with dots (more numerous in the males). The fins of the male are also more markedly colored with blue. The female has a black ocellus on the top of the root of her tail. Distinguishing the sexes is therefore very easy.

The male closing in on the female in anticipation of a possible spawning if she decides not to move further.

Egg-laying tooth carps generally spawn on plants but in the absence of such plant cover they spawn anywhere regardless of the type of substrate. Photos by R. Zukal.

For breeding purposes this species does not require special considerations. The size of the spawning aquarium should be two and a half gallon capacity or smaller for easy retrieval of the breeders or the eggs. A tank cover is imperative because these fish are known for their jumping abilities and they can find the smallest space or crack to get through. A moderate amount of plant material, preferably a bushy or filamentous type, is needed where the eggs can be deposited. It will also serve as an additional barrier in case the *Rivulus* attempt to jump out of the water. The water should be soft and slightly acid with a temperature of 76° to 78°F, more or less similar to the temperature in its native range. The maintenance of a relatively uniform temperature is important since spawning will certainly be affected by sudden

The male "dancing" within sight of the female. Photo by R. Zukal.

The chase proceeds as below, both fish seem to have found the spot to spawn. Photo by R. Zukal.

temperature changes and death may even occur if the temperature rises above 95° or below 60°F. However these fish are hardy and generally survive such accidents provided the temperature is raised gradually. Lowering the depth of the water facilitates the process of heating the water without further injury to the fish since a smaller volume of water requires less time to heat.

For breeding select the best looking pair in your stock, the female with a well rounded abdomen and the most active and brilliantly colored male. Once by themselves in the the confines of the small breeding tank it does not take too long for spawning to take place. The eggs are laid singly on the foliage of the plants towards the surface, on the bottom, on top of the gravel, or any place that suits them. After three days the amount of eggs laid diminishes and the breeders may be removed since they will not hesitate eating the eggs or the hatching fry. But if enough food is available the eggs may escape predation and the parents may be removed as

He presses the female into the plants where she lays an egg or two which is fertilized immediately. Photo by R. Zukal.

The paler female fish at the right is half buried in the vegetation as the male keeps his curved body very close to her. (Below) The spawning over they start to move on elsewhere. Photos by R. Zukal.

The pair preparing to spawn this time in the rocky part of the tank and below, the male pressing his body on the side of the female. Photos by R. Zukal.

Despite the awkward location the male places his full weight on the female as they spawn and below, body still curved, he moves away. Photos by R. Zukal.

much as 10 days after spawning. One can also pick out the eggs carefully and transfer them, with the aid of a pipette, into another tank with similar water conditions each day. However do not pick them too soon after laying to avoid possible injury to the developing egg. A better method is to transfer the plants with the eggs as a unit to another aquarium.

The eggs hatch into fairly large fry after 12 to 14 days from the time of spawning and they tend to stay close to the surface. Not very many eggs hatch as a rule so spawning several pairs at one time ensures a greater supply of young. Small-sized live food such as *Daphnia*, mosquito larvae, Enchytraed worms, are taken eagerly. Live foods are preferred but if sufficiently starved they learn to accept prepared dried foods as well. They do better, however, on live foods, especially brine shrimp nauplii.

Two weeks after hatching they can be transferred to a larger tank. It takes 5 to 9 months for the young to reach sexual maturity although for best results the breeders should at least be a year old.

A pair spawning beneath a log. Whatever eggs are laid should be picked up with a pipette daily. Photo by R. Zukal.

Body color pattern, size and shape of fins are important points of consideration in breeding fancy guppies. This yellow snakeskin was bred by Foo Phang Ting in Singapore, 1972. Photo by Dr. H. R. Axelrod.

The Guppy
Poecilia reticulata Peters 1859

It will indeed be hard to find a person who may not have heard of the guppy. They are so readily available, inexpensive, and easy to keep and breed that inevitably they become recommended "first" fish for almost all beginning aquarists. However, this is not the end of their usefulness. The guppy, along with the platies, mollies and swordtails, belongs to the family Poeciliidae and, except for one subfamily, all poeciliids are livebearers. As such they are interesting fishes and have been the subject of experiments and research by physiologists, geneticists, evolutionists and behaviorists. Due to its voracious appetite for insect larvae the guppy has been utilized as a means of controlling mosquitoes.

The wild male guppy is colorful with attractive body markings which have definite functions during courtship.

The female guppy is distinctly larger than the male but less colorful. These are 1945 quality fancy guppies. Photo by M. F. Roberts.

A male gold guppy starting to court a passing female. He is occupied with chasing females most of the time. Photo by R. Zukal.

The guppy originated in the fresh and brackish streams of northern Brazil, Guyana, Venezuela and in the Barbados and Trinidad Islands. Through the years it has been introduced in many areas and they are now known growing in the wilds of every temperate and tropical continent in the world.

Although the wild, common guppy is well known for its capacity to endure wide ranges of conditions, one tries to maintain the optimum conditions in order to get the most out of the fancy guppy varieties. In temperate areas guppies can pass winter even in an unheated tank as low as 65°F. but they may fail to survive temperatures lower than 50°F. A water temperature between 68° and 80°F. is satisfactory for keeping and breeding fancy guppies. For convenience and economy medium sized aquaria (10–20 gallons) are adequate. Crowding can inhibit the growth but too few fishes in a large tank is wasteful and not necessary.

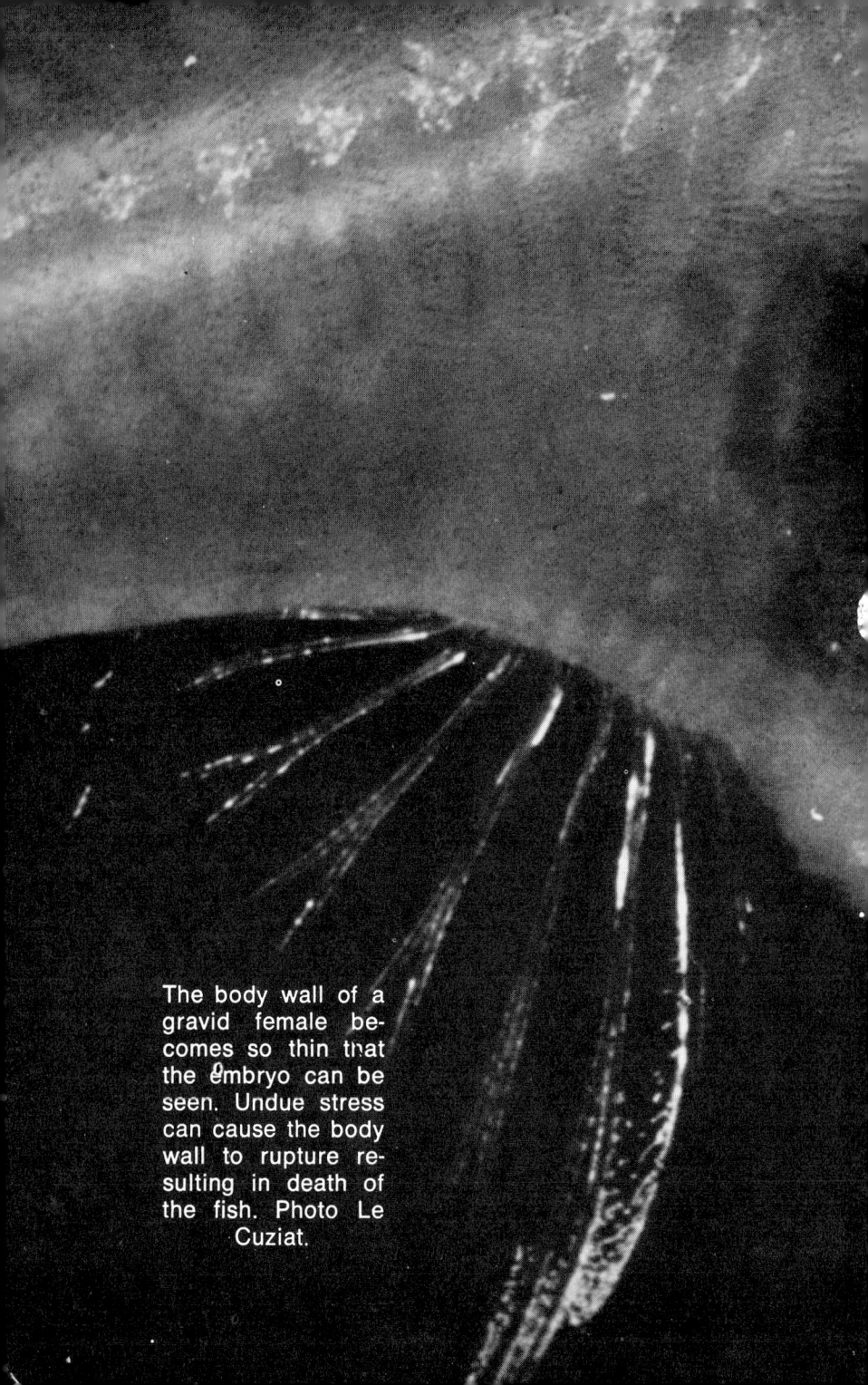

The body wall of a gravid female becomes so thin that the embryo can be seen. Undue stress can cause the body wall to rupture resulting in death of the fish. Photo Le Cuziat.

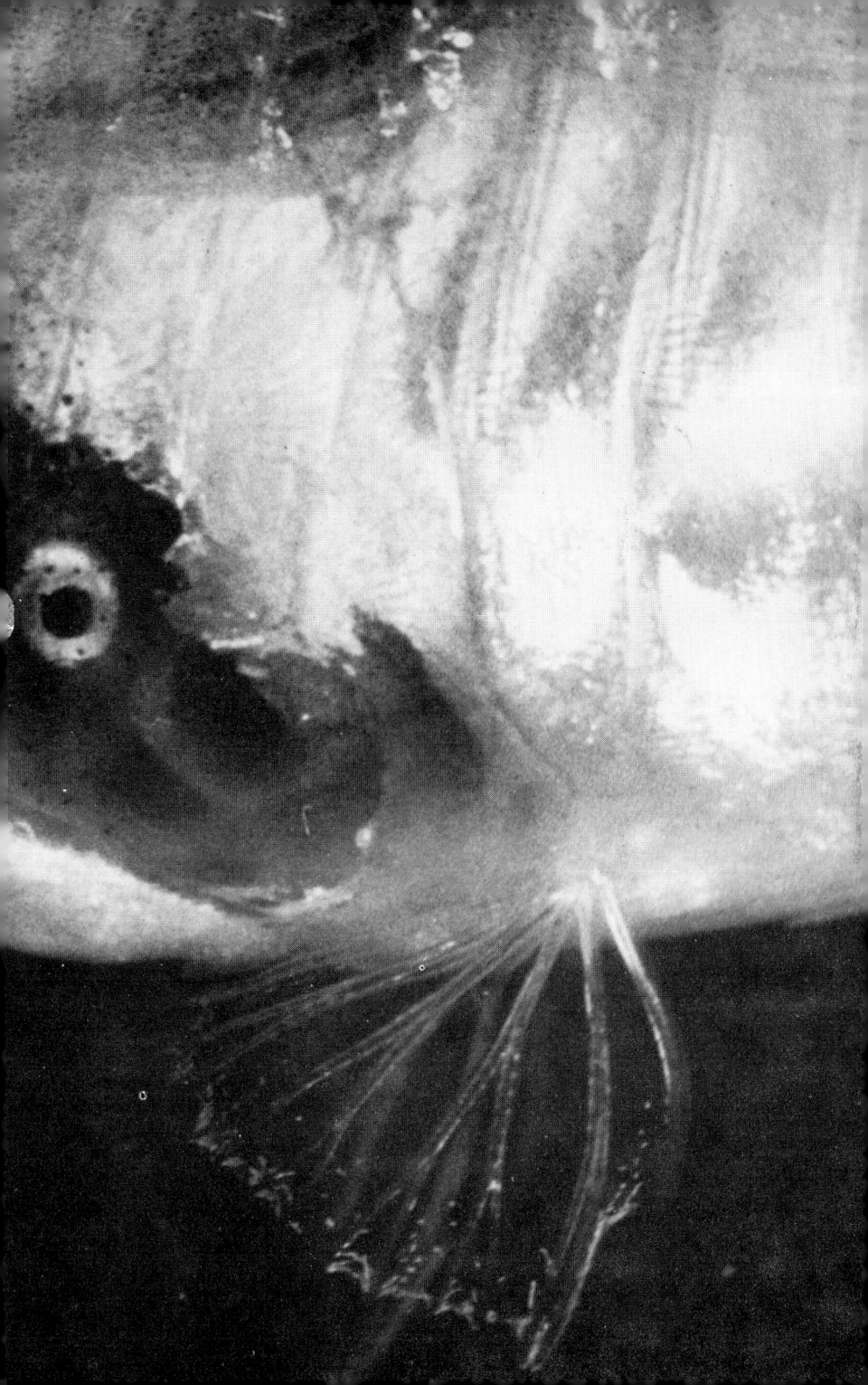

A male with well-marked but still normal-sized fins and gonopodium. Undue lengthening of these structures detracts greatly from their normal functions. 1950 Fancy Guppy.

Like most fishes dependent on gill respiration (labyrinths are able to obtain oxygen from the atmosphere), the amount of available oxygen in the water is critical. Aeration plays an important role particularly in a densely populated tank. Overfeeding, which is so common among anxious beginners, can result in fouling the water leading to oxygen depletion. Excess food together with other detrital accumulations should always be removed periodically. Overcrowding should be avoided. A lesser number of healthy fishes is much better than an excess of sick and dying guppies.

Water hardness is not very critical but extreme amounts of minerals are not desirable. Water of medium hardness (6–10 DH) is recommended. As mentioned above guppies inhabit brackish water in the wild and may even survive in sea water provided the transition is gradual, though the addition of salt water even if introduced gradually is not wise. The best salinity range is between 500 to 1,000 parts per million. The addition of a level teaspoon of rock salt to a gallon of tap water roughly produces a salinity of 1,000 parts per million. A pH between 6.5 and 7.0 is reasonable for any guppy. Again the extremes are best avoided.

Guppies are omnivorous, they eat both animal and plant food. The natural animal food is mostly insect larvae and crustaceans. They are quite happy with *Tubifex*, *Artemia*, *Daphnia*, *Cyclops* and mosquito larvae and they accept dry foods also. To complete the diet chopped spinach or other vegetable material may be given. Freeze-dried foods are a real treat.

Without doubt guppies can be kept in a bare tank satisfactorily but in order to show one's prized guppies to the

Breeding several males with one female is not wise if one were interested in preserving a particular set of known characters in the progeny. 1960 Fancy Guppy.
Photo by R. Zukal.

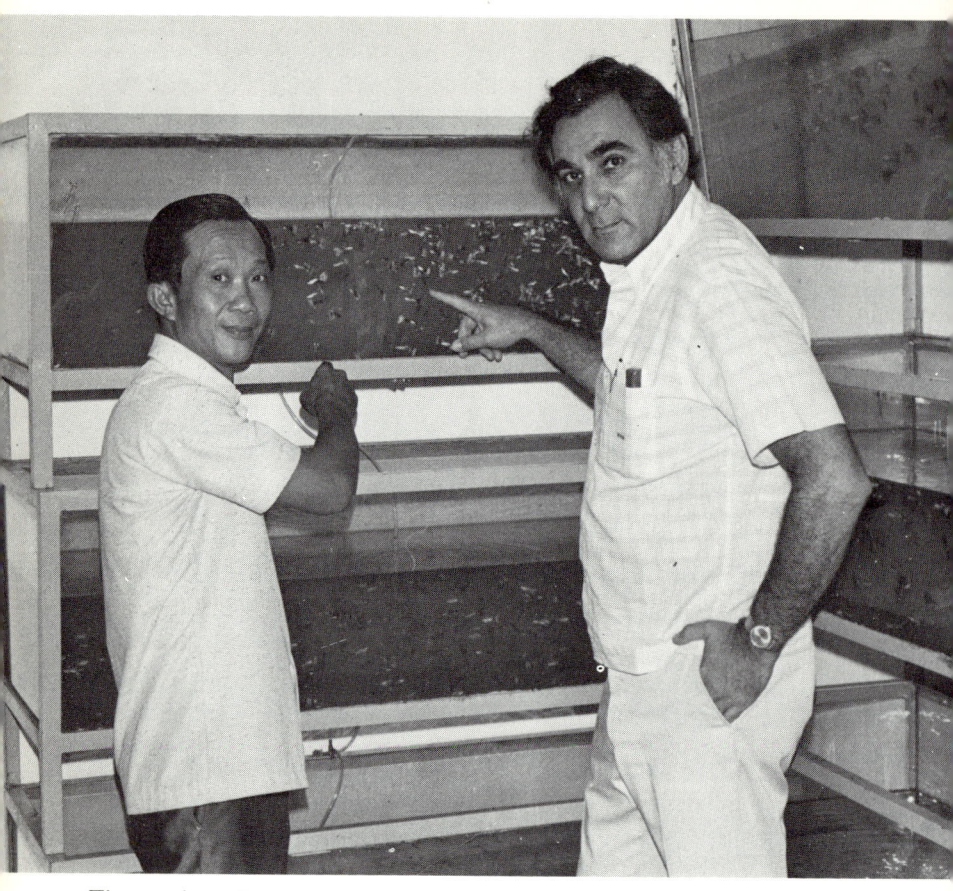

The author, Dr. Herbert R. Axelrod, with Foo Phang Ting, one of Singapore's most successful breeders and winner of many guppy awards.

greatest advantage the presence of a gravel substrate, some plants and a few rocks or stones provide a more natural setting than a bare aquarium.

Just like any other species one selects the parents with care. There are many varieties of domesticated guppies available commercially, from fancy guppy breeders, pet shops or from members of guppy associations. The selection is so wide that choice is only limited by personal preference. The males of both the wild and domesticated forms are much smaller and definitely more colorful than the females. The females of earlier stocks of guppies were less colorful with a few spots in the tail and some colored iridescent scales on the sides of the body. However, through selection and breeding, and in some cases by hormone treatment, colorful females were produced and are available now. Males are easily identified also by the presence of the gonopodium or copulatory organ found in most live-bearers.

A close-up view of the gonopodium of the male guppy. Photo Le Cuziat.

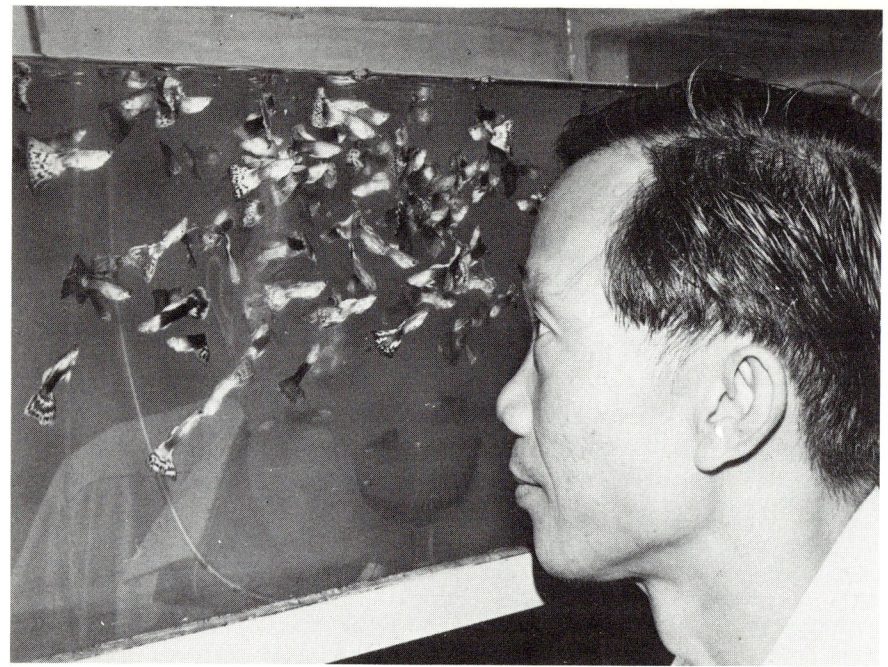

Foo Phang Ting with a tankful of male guppies rejected for breeding but offered for export from Singapore through the firm of Y. W. Ong.

With a separating glass panel one can conserve tank space and at the same time isolate and precondition the selected female (preferably a previously un-mated or virgin fish) and male prior to spawning in the same tank.

Courtship in guppies is an elaborate affair with the male performing the greater role. In a tank where both males and females are kept together, the males are mostly occupied chasing and courting the females, in constant search for a willing female. One can expect the same type of activity in a pair of guppies intended for breeding. The male approaches the female from behind and he chases her for some time until he confronts her, directly pausing in front of her. Then he turns away from her but at the same time making S-shaped motions as if to hold her attention further. If the

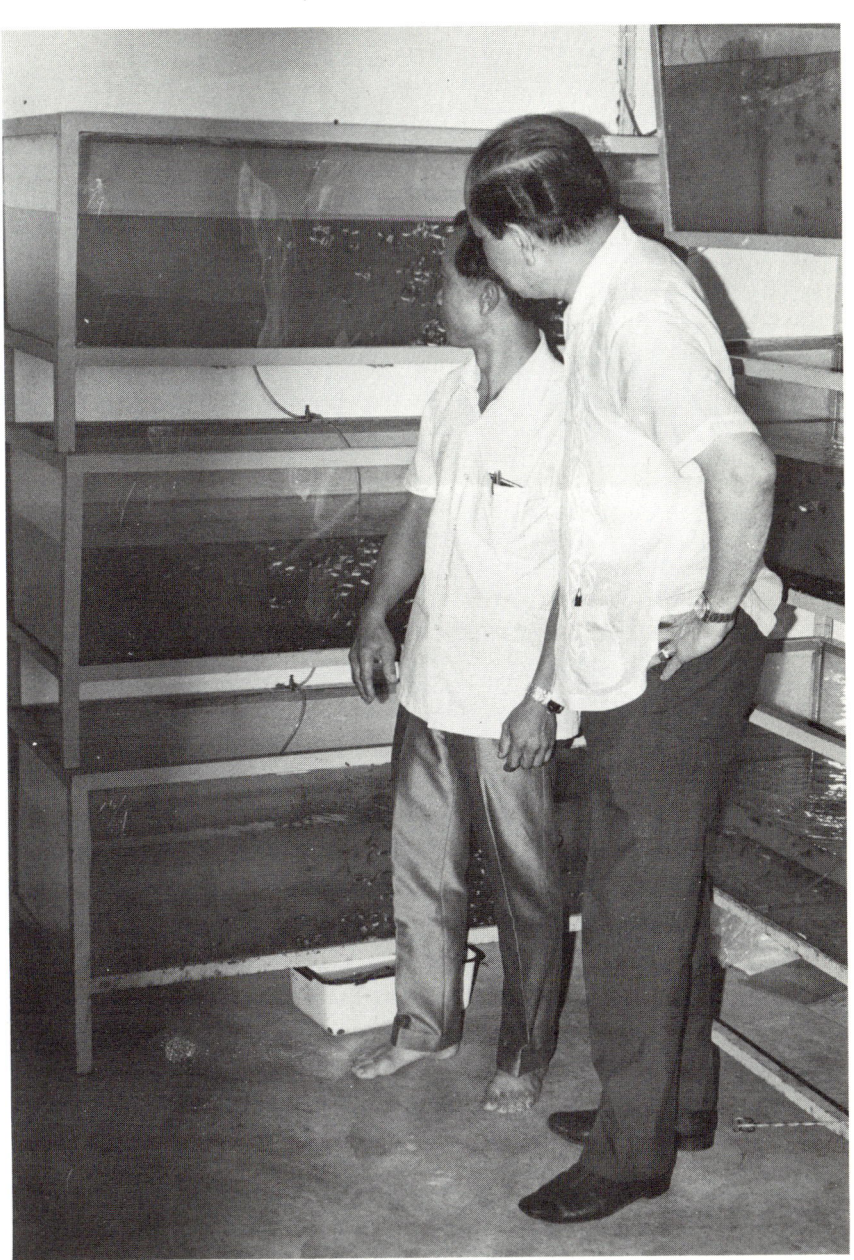

Y. W. Ong, Singapore's leading fish specialist, buys thousands of guppies annually from Foo Phang Ting. The guppies are maintained in naked tanks.

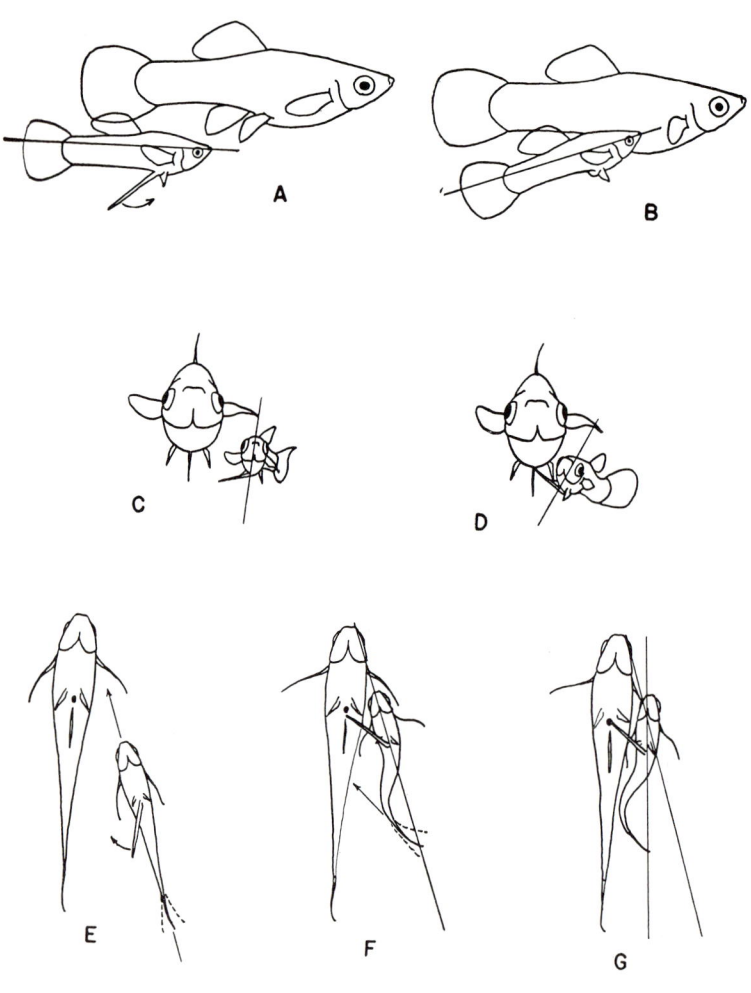

Diagrammatic representation of insemination in the guppy above, and the process of rotating the gonopodium in the male guppy, opposite page. Drawings courtesy of the late Dr. Myron Gordon.

female is receptive, she follows him and keeps on swimming until they are parallel to each other. Then the male positions himself transversely before her and displays some more by extending his tail fin; his spots and body color appear more intense. He soon makes a loop by swimming behind her and turning back below her abdominal region to effect a contact between his extended gonopodium and the genital pore of the female. Normally the gonopodium, which is the male's modified anal fin, is directed backwards but during mating it is pointed forward. In association with some rays of the pelvic fins it forms a groove through which the spermatophore (a compact bundle of sperm cells) is introduced into the genital opening of the female. The tip of the gonopodium also bears hook-like processes to insure penetration and attachment for a short few seconds. Copulation is not always successful so the courtship ritual is repeated several times. A successful contact lasts about 5 seconds. Out of hundreds of "passes" successful copulations may number less than ten! The male can be removed after the mating.

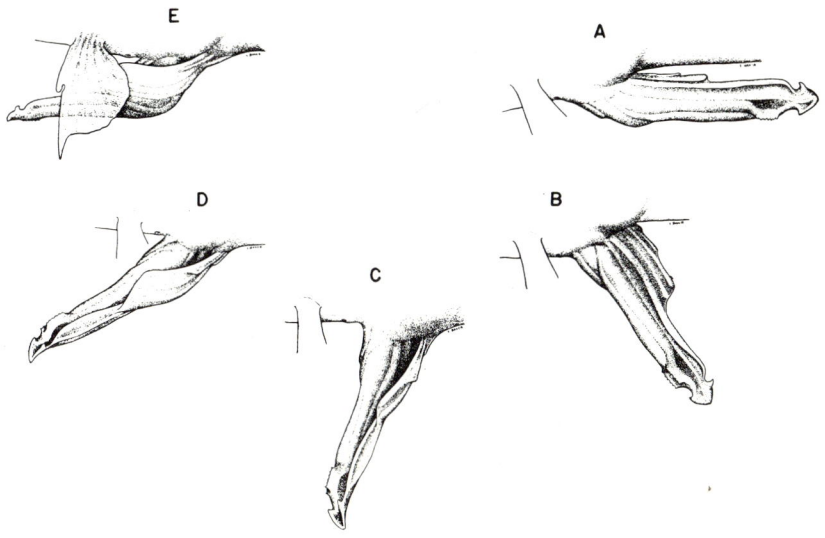

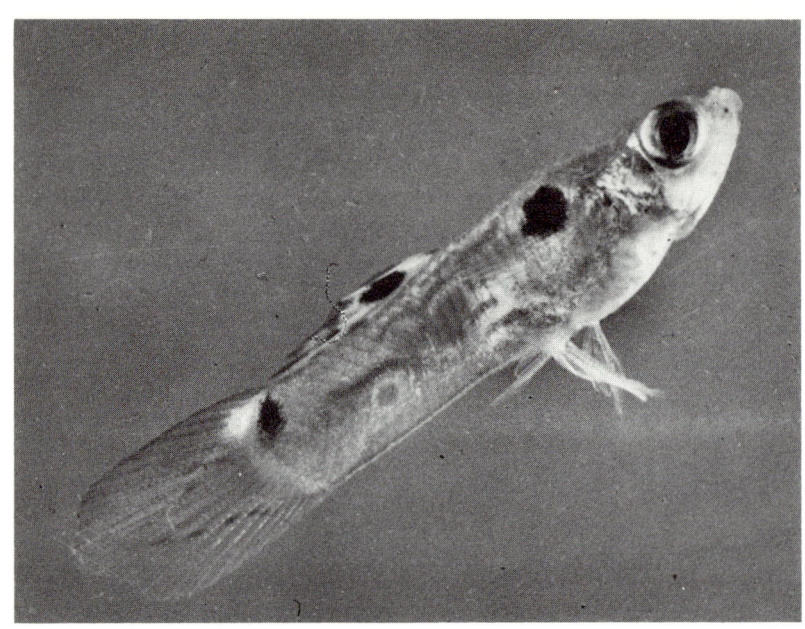

Male guppy with the gonopodium extended half-way and below in full forward position.

Male guppy with gonopodium deflected forwards approaches the female from the rear and below, ready to mate, with the gonopodium turned laterally for insertion.

The sperm cells are retained in the folds of the genital tract of the female and several successive monthly batches of eggs can be fertilized, resulting in a succession of broods. For this reason it is not wise to use more than one male at one time nor mate the same female to a different male too soon. Using only virgin females precludes getting fry of unknown male parentage. Depending on the temperature and other conditions such as light and food, the gestation

If successfully inserted a packet of sperm cells travels through the gonopodium into the female genital tract.

Female guppy "giving birth" to its young one after the other.
Photos by C. Milan.

period lasts about 4 to 6 weeks. Females in the last stages of pregnancy should be handled carefully. She could drop her young prematurely and be fatally hurt.

Relative to the size and age a female guppy can give birth to a brood of 20 to 100 fry or in rare cases even 200. They are released still encased by a delicate membrane which is removed as the fry uncoils immediately upon release or seconds later as it drops down towards the bottom. Sometimes within two minute time intervals three fishes are born. They swim actively and being phototropic will move towards the most lighted part of the tank. They start feeding immediately. Unfortunately they can easily become the food of the mother or any other fish in the tank. In spite of the many devices used by guppy breeders like funnels, "guppy traps," mosquito nettings, etc., it appears that a good plant

With a rapid flick of the tail the fry escapes from its membranous casing. Photo by Milan Chvojka.

Two fry being released almost simultaneously and below, the released fry swimming right away. Photos by Milan Chvojka.

Many of the fry end up as food of the hungry mother. Photo by M. F. Roberts.

A fry already free of its membrane emerging head first. Photo by F. M. Williams.

Some guppy embryos almost ready to be born, having been surgically removed from a dead female.
Photo by Dr. A. van den Nieuwenhuizen.

Male hormones can bring color out in females.

By proper selection and hybridization guppy breeders produce strains that are as desirable as the double-sword.
Photo by F. M. Roberts, 1960.

cover like *Nitella, Myriophyllum* and other fine-leafed plants provide a barrier which is not only effective but more natural in appearance also. The fry can easily go through dense mass of plants while the adult is unable to pursue them. When all the fish in a litter are released the female can be removed and one can expect the next brood to emerge 30 days later at a temperature of 75°F. under good lighting and food conditions.

Overcrowding can easily ruin the delicate tails of veiltail guppies. Photo by Dr. H. R. Axelrod of 1972 Foo Phang Ting fish.

Different color varieties of veiltail guppies from Singapore, 1970.

A female guppy surrounded by different male varieties, 1932. From W. T. Innes.

Two male wild guppies showing the characters of the wild form of *Poecilia reticulata*. Photo by Dr. H. R. Axelrod.

This fancy male yellow veiltail snakeskin guppy could only survive in the aquarium. In the wild it can not compete with other faster swimming fish. Photo by Dr. H. R. Axelrod of Foo Phang Ting fish, 1972.

Even in tank-bred forms the male guppy like the snakeskin lyretail guppy is more colorful than the female, 1968. Photo by R. Zukal.

Some guppy forms are prized not for an attractive color pattern but for the absence of any pattern as this gold flamingo strain. Photo by R. Zukal.

Unless one is involved in large-scale guppy breeding it is probably not imperative to prepare special guppy baby formula. The young can be fed newly-hatched brine shrimp and micro-worms together with a mixture of powdered dried foods.

The fry can be kept in a 10 or 20 gallon aquarium for a month or so. They grow rapidly and are sexually mature in two months but reach full growth in six months. As soon as they are sexable it is reasonable to segregate them according to sex to prevent early matings. Only full-grown fish should be mated, except in certain varieties with over-developed gonopodiums. They are best mated earlier since successful copulation is not possible due to their abnormal copulatory organ which develops later in their lives!

A veiltail guppy in almost perfect condition. Photo by M. Hill, 1971.

The extremely long gonopodium of this guppy precludes normal reproduction at this stage. Photo by H. Hansen, 1971.

The Tiger or Zebra Cichlid
Tilapia mariae Boulenger

This member of the large genus *Tilapia* of the cichlid family is distributed in West Africa in the delta of the Niger, lagoons and shallow areas along the Ivory Coast south to Cameroon. Presently it is one of the many African imports that has become popular among aquarists. They are easy to keep and very prolific with a very interesting life history.

The size of the brood of this guarding tiger cichlid reflects the fecundity of most *Tilapia* species. Photo by G. Marcuse.

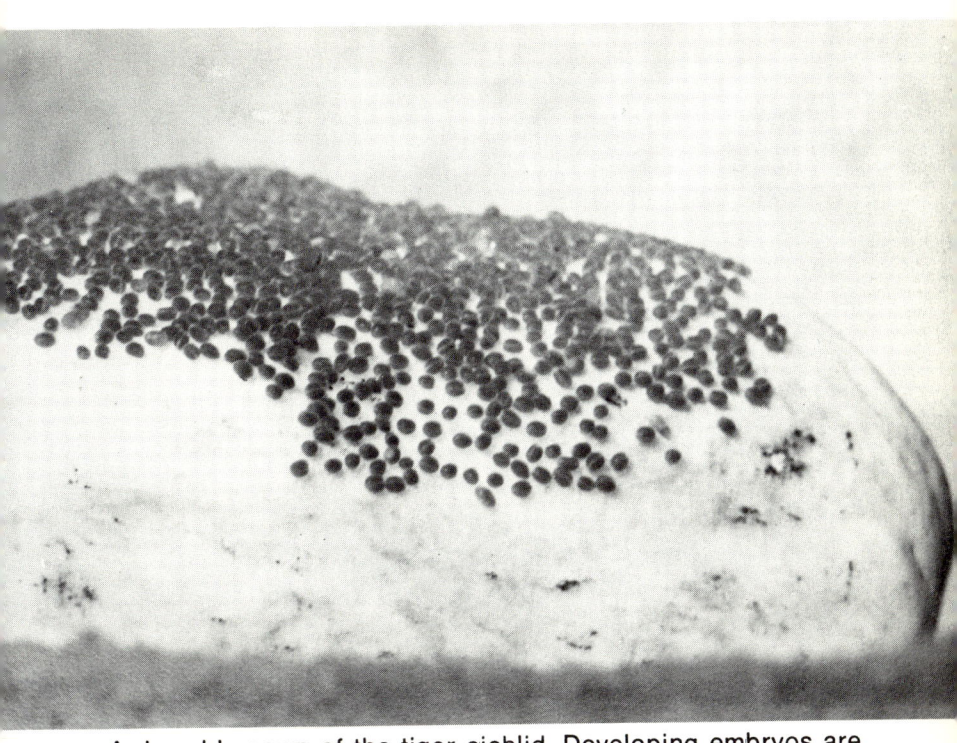

A day-old spawn of the tiger cichlid. Developing embryos are already discernable. Photo by G. Marcuse.

Since they can grow to five inches in length while in captivity (in the wild eight inches) they should be kept in fairly large aquaria. Although they are territorial only during breeding time and less aggressive in other phases of life, in the aquarium they tend to stay aggressive towards other fishes and even other smaller individuals of their own kind. So, they are best left alone by themselves and the weaker members separated or isolated. They can tolerate a wide range of water conditions, slight changes in pH and hardness are not critical but a water temperature between 72° and 85°F. should be maintained. They are not very selective feeders and will accept most of the usual aquarium fare but their diet should be supplemented with vegetable matter (algae, spinach, lettuce). The presence of some flat rocks

Parents take turns guarding the eggs. Photo by G. Marcuse.

The barred condition of the young is not completely lost in the adult stage. Photo by Dr. H. R. Axelrod.

The hatched fry are moved from the egg site to a shallow pit and guarded by the parent *T. mariae*. Photo by G. Marcuse.

upon a coarse sand or fine gravel bottom will fulfill the requirements for spawning. Including some plants, no matter how well anchored, will prove futile since they will be uprooted and eaten. If for aesthetic reasons they are desired, plastic plants will serve the purpose but they really should be firmly anchored . . . Even cemented to the floor of the aquarium.

The common names Tiger and Zebra Cichlid refer to the appearance of the barred young *T. mariae*. The basic color

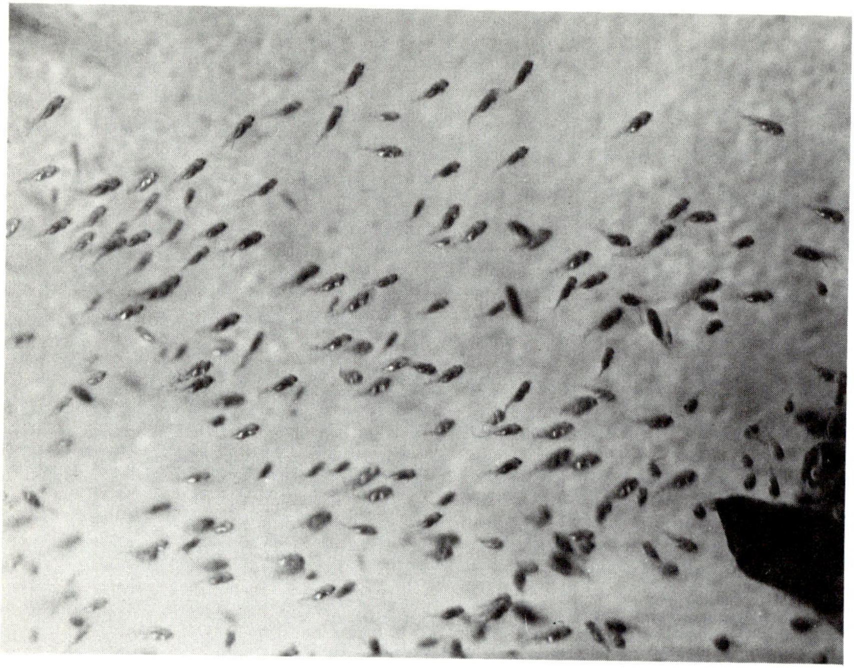

The fry in various stages of development: newly hatched facing page, top; 3 days old, facing page, bottom; three weeks, above.

is yellow with several wide black/brown bands across the body including one across the eye. As the young fish mature the stripes disappear although not completely, for several dark very distinct blotches remain along the sides of the body. The body color remains yellowish turning greenish towards the back and the head. Small red spots develop on the fins and in the center of some scales of the back.

Two-week old fry still instinctively bound with the parent fish.
Photos by G. Marcuse.

(Facing page) Two-week old fry ready to leave the pit. Below,
facing page: The parent fish "calling" the young.

The zebra-like marking is fully developed in the 10-week old fry shown here milling about the parents.
Photos by G. Marcuse.

There are reports that a completely black form of *T. mariae* exists among the usual adult spotted form in natural populations. It is completely black except for a very narrow red stripe along the upper edge of the dorsal and caudal fins. One authority explains that the black or melanistic form represents the non-breeding phase of the species.

On the basis of color the sexes are indistinguishable but the genital papilla of the male is conical and that of the female is truncate or without an apex. The fins of the male are also slightly longer.

This species is not a mouthbrooder like the well studied mouthbrooding *T. macrochir* but is classified as a substrate brooder. They do not build nests. Spawning is simple, without courtship rituals. The male and female fish merely associate near the spawning site. In nature tiger cichlids prefer to deposit the eggs underneath large stones. Hence they have to spawn upside down! In such protected areas they lay between 200 to 400 eggs. Each egg measures about 1.8 mm in diameter. The eggs are laid along a wide circle a few at a time and each batch fertilized by the male hovering close by. More and more eggs are added towards the center until the whole area is filled. In captivity, where conditions are different, the eggs are laid on the surface of stones, at times haphazardly. Both parents guard the eggs. The female takes care of the housekeeping, cleaning and fanning the eggs while the male takes charge of driving off any intruder coming too close. It has been observed in *T. mariae* that prior to hatching of the eggs, the female moves the eggs to a new site (a depression on the bottom) prepared earlier. Dead or infertile eggs are left behind and eaten later by the female.

In two to three days the eggs hatch into larvae depending upon the temperature. During this period the larvae still have yolk sacs and they are loosely attached to the substrate by means of "head glands" (temporary organs in the head which secrete string-like mucus filaments for attachment).

Adult *T. mariae*, with its barred brood. Photo by G. Marcuse.

(Facing page) Juvenile *T. mariae*, barred in early juvenile stage. Photo by Dr. K. Knaack. Transforming juvenile *T. mariae*, lower photo.

After four weeks it is best to transfer the brood into larger tanks preferably in out-door pools if the weather permits. Photo by G. Marcuse.

Meanwhile the female still continues "brooding" above the excavation with the male warding off intruders. The yolk sac is usually absorbed after five to six days and the head filaments are detached so the young fish are free and will start swimming as a shoal. Both parents herd the fish as they all swim about but as the fish grow bigger the shoal splits into smaller groups while feeding at the bottom.

The fry at the time of hatching and onwards will accept *Artemia* nauplii, other live small food and some vegetable material also. After 24 days they are about 17 mm long; after 45 to 50 days they could be 30 mm; thereafter the parents gradually lose interest.

The Indian Glass Fish
Chanda ranga Hamilton-Buchanan

A very common fish in India, known scientifically since 1822, is the glass fish, *Chanda ranga*. This fish is also known as *Ambassis lala*, but the name doesn't mean it's a different fish so we'll leave the nomenclature to the specialists and discuss the breeding.

It is easy to understand why *Chanda ranga* are popularly called glass fish. Photo by C. Milan.

Male glassfish are easily recognized by the white edged vertical fins. Younger glassfish appear more transparent than adults having less pigmentation and color. Photos by R. Zukal.

(Above) Spawning is preceded by the inevitable chase that takes the fish to all parts of the tank. (Below) The male glass fish also develops a dark dorsal fin in the adult stage. Photos by R. Zukal.

(Above) The male approaching the female slightly sideways. (Facing page) The female catching the attention of the male. The interested female following the male towards the bushy plants. Photos by R. Zukal.

I recognize this species because I have bred them by the millions in Florida merely by throwing a few hundred into a large dirt pool and letting nature take its course. The pool may measure 25 × 100 feet, with a maximum depth of 8 feet in the center. There are a few plants along the edge of the pool, but nothing very dense. Before I put the breeders into the pool, I pump the pool as dry as possible, and then cover the bottom and sides with hydrated powdered lime. This kills all the harmful organisms in the ooze at the bottom, and acts as a fertilizing base as the pool fills with ground water. Within a two-week period the pool has filled itself and the water has become crystal

The body of the glass fish is so transparent that very few parts of the internal anatomy remain hidden from view. Photo by Dr. H. R. Axelrod.

A dark background can enhance the transparency of the glass fish. Photo by Dr. K. Knaack.

clear. I then add some cottonseed meal and cow manure, a few pounds of each, and this turns the water brown, at which time life appears in the pool in the form of clouds of *Cyclops* and *Daphnia*. At this time I put in my breeder glass fish, using about 50% males to females.

The males are fairly easy to identify because they have a white edging on their second dorsal and anal fins, while the female does not have this characteristic coloring. There is a difference in the position and size of their swim bladders, clearly seen through the semi-transparent flesh.

In pool breeding, the fish spawn and the fry develop without problems from the breeders. In an aquarium it is quite another story. Pairs should be conditioned separately and their spawning tank should be set up with dense

In spite of its delicate appearance glassfish are not difficult to keep. Photo by R. Zukal.

Once within the bushes the male positions himself beside the female and within a few moments they spawn accompanied by body quivering and fin flapping. Upon completion of spawning the parents should be removed for they will actively hunt eggs to eat. Photos by R. Zukal.

bunches of spawning grass in one end. These fish like lots of heat, and 90° is an ideal spawning temperature for them. The water I used in Florida was very hard, alkaline water, but in the aquarium this kind of water kills them! So try neutral, soft water and see if you get good results. If the fish keeps its fins clamped, then it is obviously not very happy about what is going on, so you'd better change the water chemistry a bit. Water is the most important problem with glass fish; temperature is also very important, so keep it high at all times. Never allow it to fall below 80°.

The breeders, when placed into the spawning tank, will chase each other into the spawning grass where they will spray their eggs among the fine leaves. The eggs are fairly sticky and will number about 200 if the pair are properly

As soon as these fishes lose interest with each other they start eating the eggs and they should then be removed. Photo by G. J. M. Timmerman.

seasoned. Use a strong light to shine on the eggs as they are very tiny and transparent and they are easily missed if you have never seen them before. If you use a glass bottom spawning tank (five gallons is large enough), shine a light up from the bottom and the eggs appear as small, shiny beads.

Remove the parents as soon as they have spawned or they begin an egg hunt and will devour their own spawn in short order. The eggs hatch in a little more than a day and in four days the fry are free swimming and looking for food. This is the critical stage: unless they have copious amounts of infusoria they starve. Unfortunately they are too small for newly hatched brine shrimp until they are two weeks old.

American flagfish are best maintained in a well-planted aquarium. Photo by Dr. H. R. Axelrod of a colorful male.

American Flagfish

Jordanella floridae Goode & Bean, 1879

Jordanella floridae, commonly known as the American Flagfish, is the only known species of egg-laying tooth carps (family Cyprinodontidae) that takes care of its young. The species is widely distributed in Florida, especially in the southern parts. The flagfish is normally found in marshes, ponds, lakes, and streams throughout its range and not uncommonly in shallow irrigation ditches and canals along the roads.

This fish has been ignored by most fish dealers, probably being considered as a usual, common type of fish with few redeeming qualities such as having a bold or striking pattern or exhibiting any unusual or interesting behavior. It has however, always been coveted by European aquarists,

The color pattern of *Jordanella* is very variable and is greatly influenced by the physiological and psychological state of the fish. Photos by V. Elek.

The male American flagfish normally prepares the nesting site and lures the female to spawn in it. Photo by V. Elek.

particularly the Germans, who deplore the fact that very few individuals reach their local stores, although it was first imported into Germany as early as 1914.

Though their color pattern is variable the flagfish are basically olive-green with a checkerboard pattern of dark stripes and spots of reddish color. Both sexes exhibit a distinct black spot on the side which is more pronounced in the female. The female is also reported to have a black spot edged with white at the base of the end of the dorsal fin. During the non-breeding stage the flagfish appear rather drab in color. During the breeding season however, the male is transformed into an attractive, brilliantly colored fish with iridescent spots of all the colors of the rainbow. The pattern of the female also becomes more intense during breeding but hardly reaches the brilliancy of the males. Finding them in

Note the two transparent eggs just released by the female. Photo by V. Elek.

their Florida habitat at this time is facilitated by merely observing any flashes of bright coloration in the shallow water among the plants close to the edge of the stream.

It is not difficult to duplicate the conditions found in their natural habitat and *Jordanella floridae* can be expected to breed in captivity without much trouble. Being sub-tropical in distribution, this species requires warm temperature and hard water similar to those of its biotope. Flagfish can tolerate or survive temperatures as low as 45°F. but will not spawn until the temperatures reach about 70°F. or higher. The addition of sea water (1 gallon of sea water to each five gallons of fresh water) or appropriate synthetic salts and a pH of about 7.5 or higher should help to initiate a spawning situation.

The aquarium (8 to 10 gallon capacity) should be provided with well-secured plants which can give adequate protection to the female during the nuptial chase and also places where the spawn may be attached in the usual cyprinodont manner. Some clear areas should be left at the bottom of the tank as the flagfish are known to dig shallow depressions in the substrate, cichlid fashion, for their nest. The latter is usually chosen by the female.

The male hovering about the spawning female.
Photo by V. Elek.

After a turbulent courtship the female who is also at times more aggressive will lay small batches of eggs (about 25 in each group) daily for several days to a week. At about 75°F. the young hatch five to six days after spawning. The young are led about by the male cichlid style. The female is best removed after the young fish have appeared although this is not always necessary. In nature the male is very protective of the nest. He guards and fans the eggs diligently and he establishes a well-defined territory and any intruder, including the female and other neighboring flagfish that are also spawning are quickly chased off. Within the confines of the aquarium the male may not be as pugnacious as those in the wild and if the eggs were scattered and not laid in the nests he may ignore them completely and the females are hardly molested at times. By observing the behavior of one

The male with body curved and touching the female now fertilizing the batch of eggs just laid. Can you see the eggs? Photo by V. Elek.

Top view of a spawning pair of American flagfish as they S-curve. Photo by V. Elek.

parent towards the other one can decide whether it is necessary to remove the female.

When the male flagfish loses interest in caring for the young the latter may be transferred into a tank of their own. Adult *Jordanella floridae* thrive well on both live food, such as *Daphnia*, cyclops, etc., and dried, prepared foods. They keep best when their diet is supplemented with vegetable matter. The flagfish is omnivorous in nature. The newly hatched fry are large and will be able to eat the nauplii of brine shrimp and fine algae (chopped vegetables such as spinach and lettuce are acceptable substitutes).

It only takes about 3 months for the fry to reach sexual maturity. Keep the sexes separate, if possible, prior to spawning.

The delicate beauty of Schaller's gourami has been captured by these excellent pictures by H. J. Richter, above and by E. Roloff, on the facing page.

Schaller's Gourami

Trichopsis schalleri Ladiges

Trichopsis schalleri is the lesser known member of the genus *Trichopsis* which also includes the popular croaking gourami (*T. vittatus*) and the pygmy gourami (*T. pumilus*). Like all other anabantoids these fishes possess an accessory organ of respiration called the labyrinth which requires them to breathe atmospheric air. As they gulp or swallow

A pair of *Trichopsis vittatus*, a closely related species of *T. schalleri* guarding its nest built underneath a leaf. Photo by H. J. Richter.

air members of the genus *Trichopsis* produce an audible snapping sound as a result of which they are often called *croaking gouramis*. It is not proper to ascribe any significance to this sound production; it is simply the result of gulping air rapidly.

The coloration of this gourami is not as garish as other members of the suborder Anabantoidei (like the *Betta, Macropodus, Colisa, Trichogaster,* etc.) but subdued and delicately tinted. The body sides are brownish at the top changing to golden brown to white towards the abdomen. Two red-brown stripes run along the mid-section of the sides of the body from the head to the base of the tail. These bands become more vivid or turn dull depending on the mood of the fish. Except for the paired fins which are colorless, the unpaired fins are speckled with reddish brown and edged with reddish tinge. The caudal fin ends in a slender thread-like, short filament. Under favorable lighting the fish appears golden, the reddish brown parts appear brick red, and the scale rows shine with an iridescent

All the eggs scattered about are later mouthed and deposited into the nest below the leaf. Photo by H. J. Richter.

greenish blue lustre. The eyes are particularly pretty, ringed in red, and the iris a gleaming emerald green.

Trichopsis schalleri was originally described from aquarium specimens imported from Thailand. They are easy to keep and will be content in a well-planted, medium-sized tank (10–20 gallons) with fairly warm (80°–85°F.), soft, slightly acid water more or less similar to that found in their native habitat. Water hardness and pH are not critical. They are known to spawn even in hard water. Aeration is not necessary for maintaining adults. Subdued lighting is more natural to this fish but they spawn regardless of light conditions. Since they can be hostile to one another, especially the males during breeding time, one sees the importance of a good plant cover or other means of hiding.

Ordinarily the sexes are difficult to segregate. There are no obvious external character differences. However, at full sexual maturity, the female's abdomen is larger and by

Sex differences are not very obvious except during the breeding season. Paler fish above is the female. Photo by E. Roloff.

Catching the eggs as the embrace ends. Photo by H. J. Richter.

means of a strong light shining through the body wall the outlines of the eggs can be seen. As usual the male coloration is more vivid, too.

The male and female fish can be pre-conditioned while in isolation (easily accomplished by separating glass panes or confining each fish in a small container floated in the tank) by good and plentiful feeding with both live and prepared food. They will accept worms, brine shrimp, *Daphnia*, *Cyclops*, frozen and freeze-dried foods.

When ready to mate, as evidenced by their physical conditions and reactions to one another, they can be released into a small tank but make sure that there are some broadleafed plants like the Amazon sword plant or some clusters of *Cryptocoryne*.

Their spawning behavior resembles that described for the croaking and pygmy gouramis. They all build bubble nests underwater. The bubbles are trapped beneath the broad leaves or other submerged objects. Siamese fighters, to the contrary, form bubble nests on the surface. The courtship in *T. schalleri* is not aggressive but yet decisive. The male lightly nudges the female sideways and stays within her sight to display his expanding fins, trembling slightly and showing off his best coloration. No actual pairing takes place as the male will first have to build a rather small bubble nest (about the size of a silver dollar piece or dime) beneath one of the leaves. As soon as the nest is completed he once more pays attention to courting the female, ulti-

Mouthed eggs are now deposited into the incompletely filled nest. Photo by H. J. Richter.

The male fish positioning his body in such a way that his vent gets closer to that of the female. Photo by H. J. Richter.

mately leading her towards the nesting vicinity. If ready the female will assume an inverted position with her belly up. Meanwhile the male arches over her body pressing her in a typical anabantoid embrace. This lasts for a few seconds, accompanied by slight trembling, and two or three eggs result.

Pairing and spawning continue over a period lasting about 7 hours. Both fish gather and spit the eggs into the nest. When the eggs in the female are exhausted the male stays close to the nest and sees to it that the female cannot eat them. In about 24 hours the fry hatch out and lie in the nest. They appear like small glass slivers with black snake-like tips.

A pair of Schaller's gouramis engaged in the well known anabantoid embrace magnificently photographed by H. J. Richter.

Photo by H. J. Richter.
The guarding instinct is particularly strong during the immediate period after spawning.

Not all the eggs are expected to develop. The few eggs that appear dull, white and opaque are dead.

Photo by H. J. Richter.

A close-up photo of the fry with the yolk. Photo by H. J. Richter.

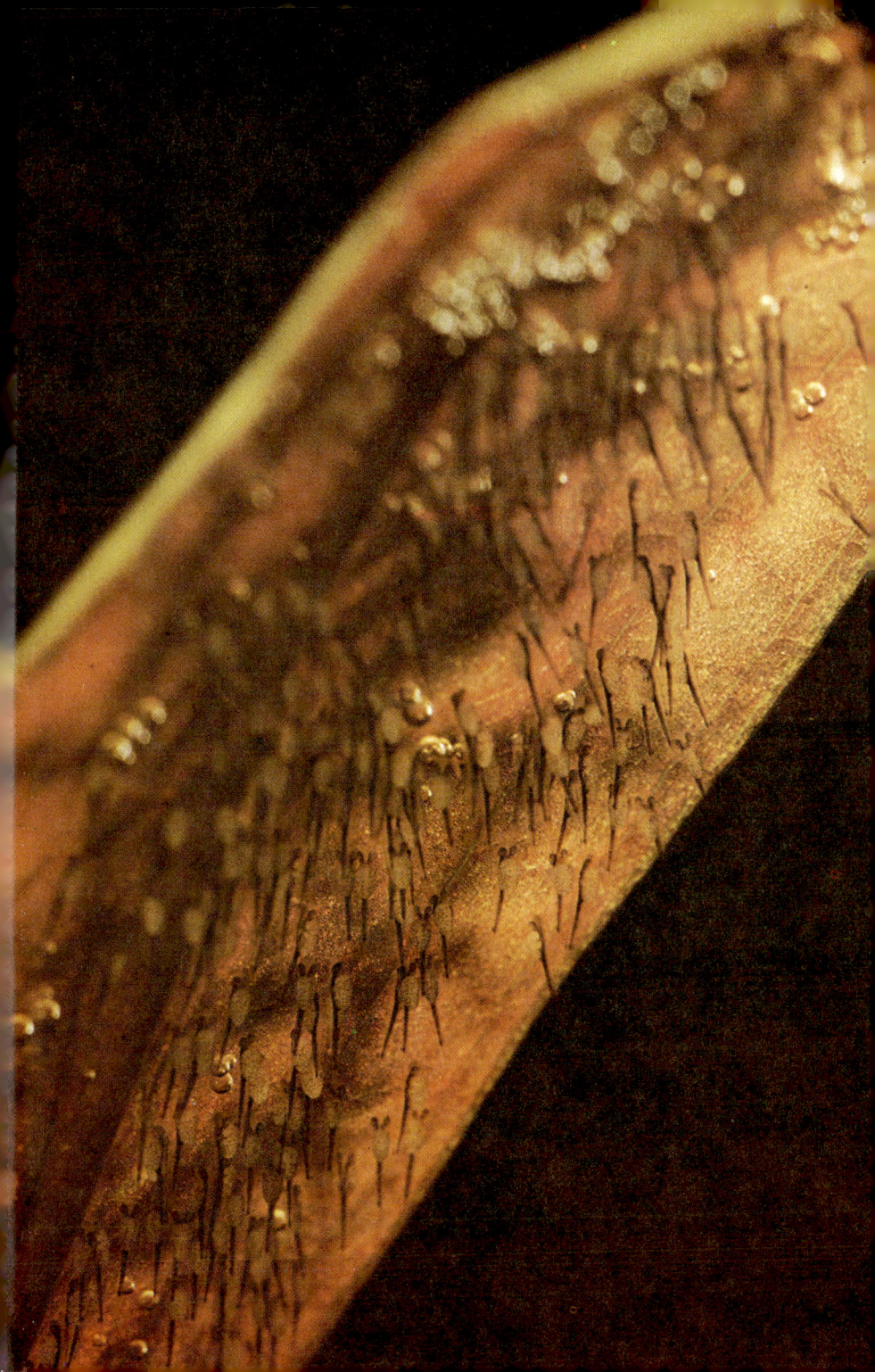

Like slivers of glass the fry of *Trichopsis* hang helplessly in the bubble nest until they hatch. Photo by H. J. Richter.

To forestall possible predation of the young by the parents it is wise to remove them both. In 36 hours the fry, still with yolk sacs, swarm out of the spawning site and hang among the plants or on the glass walls. After three days they become more active, ready to feed, as the yolk sac is now gone. The recommended food is infusoria. Macerated boiled egg yolk is also good because it favors the growth of infusoria in addition. With advancing growth they can easily tackle newly hatched brine shrimp.

Some aeration is needed for the first few weeks since the labyrinth is still not developed. This is the stage of highest mortality. At about the third week after hatching the labyrinths start functioning and they are able to start breathing atmospheric air. Color will be first noticed in the fins in about two months.

The Burundi Killy
Aphyosemion scheeli Radda

This species of killifish (family Cyprinodontidae), although fairly well known in Europe since its introduction in Germany in 1964, was not formally described until 1970 by Dr. Radda. The name "Burundi" is applied incorrectly to this species. It is inappropriate since the fish originates from West Africa (Nigeria) and not from Burundi which is in East Africa. Since the species is described in compliance with the rules of scientific nomenclature, the utilization of the name *"burundi"* as of part of the common name of *A. scheeli* is a not as objectionable as when it was used as the scientific name of an undescribed species (*nomen nudem*) before. Anyhow, the introduction of a new common name

An original photograph of *Aphyosemion scheeli* from Col. J. Scheel's book. *Rivulins of the Old World* called them "Aphyosemion burundi".

is also undesirable for it will just add more confusion to the whole matter. Thus, there is no fish named "*Aphyosemion burundi.*"

In appearance *A. scheeli* is closest to *A. gardneri,* a well known killifish and a widely distributed species (or superspecies of some systematists) in Equatorial West Africa. In fact *A. scheeli* was initially considered as a "yellow" strain of *gardneri*. The killifish expert J. Scheel* however states that this strain has lower fin ray counts and the color pattern is different. The accompanying photographs show the color and pattern of both the male and female *A. scheeli.* The basic body color of the male is blue-green to gray-green while it is more subdued or brownish in the female. The belly and the fins are distinctly yellow to orange also.

Killifishes are kept best by themselves as their fins are easily damaged. Since aggressive encounters cannot be

The presence of some plant cover is desirable to provide refuge to the Burundi killy whose fins are easily damaged by other fishes. Photo by Dr. S. Frank.

A male Burundi killy pinning the female down to the bottom. Photo by V. Elek.

avoided even amongst themselves it is wise to have a modest amount of bushy plants including some floating types amongst which they can hide. Vegetation provides hiding places, acts as a shield from too much light, too, (killies are light shy) and in this case as a barrier also for they are prone to jumping out. For added security a tank cover is needed. Being such small fish (males reach a total length of 53 mm or just over two inches) they require only small tanks (5 gallons or less). A dark sand or fine gravel bottom is appropriate. A dark bottom shows off the coloration better than a white one. The water must be soft, neutral to slightly acid, and the temperature not higher than 75°F. Aphyose-

---

* See Jørgen Scheel's *Rivulins of the Old World*. It is the most complete book on killifishes ever published.

mions are sensitive to high temperatures which can kill them at times. Keeping them in temperatures higher than that normal for the species concerned might stunt their growth and prevent the development of the best possible coloration also.

Even without one's interference these fish can spawn in a community tank anytime mature males and females are put together as a matter of course but, if you desire a batch of normal and healthy young, planning a little bit ahead might save time and work. Retrieving fishes and eggs from a large tank is cumbersome and you are far better off setting up a series of smaller tanks solely for spawning purposes. The water conditions should not be too different from the main tank, especially the temperature. As the accompanying photographs show, these fish are bottom spawners but the possibility of their scattering their eggs freely, depending upon circumstances, should not be precluded (some species

Two views of a male *A. scheeli* encouraging the female to spawn. Photos by V. Elek.

like *A. calabaricus* spawn according to the opportunities available to them). A layer of fine sand at the bottom is acceptable but if you have to pick out the eggs individually from the sand you could be spared unnecessary tedious work by simply spreading out a nylon mop at the base of the tank or a thin layer of boiled peat moss instead of using sand. These can be removed after each spawning and replaced after the eggs are taken out.

Select the best male in your stock and at least two of the best females. Never put two males together for they will spend more time fighting than attending to the business of mating. The prospective parents should be isolated and fattened up with live food *(Tubifex, Artemia, Daphnia* and mosquito larvae) for several weeks but not too long because egg binding could occur. When they are ready, as judged from their coloration and the size of their belly, place one male with at least two females in one spawning tank. Don't forget a tank cover! They get very excited during courtship and may jump out of the water.

The courtship is brief and the male forces one of the females towards the bottom where he tries to squeeze the eggs out of her. Once they lie parallel to each other spawning usually will take place. A few eggs are laid and get caught in the meshes of the spawning medium. Egg laying continues with a number of eggs laid daily. Spawning will, of course, diminish in time and ultimately stop. The spawning mop or the peat moss should be taken out every day and the water squeezed out on a towel or newspaper. The eggs then become visible and appear as small translucent spheres. They are easily picked with the fingers or with a pair of blunt-edged tweezers. Transfer the eggs into a jar preferably with a screw cap containing a bunch of boiled, damp peat

The male and female Burundi killy lying side to side are now almost ready to spawn. Photo by V. Elek.

Tail waving, body trembling and a few eggs are laid and quickly fertilized. Photo by V. Elek.

moss. You should label the jar with important data like the number of eggs and the date they were laid and set aside. The covered jar is then stored in a dark, cool place. The jars should be checked periodically for non-developing eggs. Fungused eggs appear white and fuzzy while the live ones remain plump and translucent. They should be removed before the whole batch become fungused and decomposed. Another method is to store the eggs inside small cotton bags with boiled and damp peat moss and all the individual cotton bags placed in a larger plastic bag for storage.

In about six weeks the eggs may be taken out of storage and placed in a small tank with about two inches of very soft water. Hatching should occur within a day or so. The fry are then moved to a larger aquarium. Slight agitation of the water hastens hatching and the addition of a pinch of powdered milk has been recommended in stubborn cases. The milk increases bacterial activity and the bacteria weaken the egg shell allowing the fry to burst free.

Spawning proceeds indefinitely and gradually wanes as fewer eggs are laid and the spawning frequency lessens. Photo by V. Elek.

The young can be fed with the usual small sized live food like newly hatched brine ship nauplii and microworms. High temperature and direct light should be avoided. It is known that the eggs of some species of killifish when maintained in cooler temperatures develop into more beautifully colored individuals. It appears that heat inhibits the development of pigmentation. It is also reported that the addition of some table salt improves the well-being of these fishes. Growth is slow but once they are separable it is best to separate the males from the females to avoid premature spawning. The eggs of early matings are generally smaller than those produced during full sexual development.